Praise for
THE SILENT ECHO OF MY CHILDHOOD

Sylvie Larivière-Traub's powerful and courageous introductory book reaches deep into her heart – and ours – and, in 220 pages, lays bare her life story in meticulous detail, pulling the reader into a journey of pain, loss and, in the end, redemption. Her honest, graphic, and blunt retelling of child abuse is a shocking, yet mandatory read for all who have also travelled down her road and who are in need of being heard. Sylvie's book is a triumph of the human spirit.

— Frederic Serre,
Journalist, Writer, Humorist, and Cartoonist
Montreal, Quebec
Canada

When Sylvie Larivière-Traub writes, she shows her true strength by pouring all of her heart blood, her emotions, her tears, and above all, her love onto the pages. And those pages become one of the most impressive, authentic, and touching life stories you will ever read.

— Natja Igney,
International journalist
France

Nothing short of stunning. Sylvie's story, told with raw honesty and remarkable resilience, is one of hope—a reminder that no matter the darkness, there is always a way forward. I urge you to let her story inspire you to take your own journey, to find the bravery within to recreate yourself, no matter where you begin.

— Patricia Lynn Strickland,
California Drama Director & Filmmaker
Director/Acting Teacher,
Rubicon Theatre Company 2010-2023

THE SILENT ECHO OF MY CHILDHOOD

A story of survival from foster homes and children's prison to business success

SYLVIE LARIVIÈRE-TRAUB

pink umbrella books

Copyright © 2024 by Sylvie Larivière-Traub

Printed in the United States of America

All rights reserved. No part of this publication can be reproduced, stored in a retrieval system, or transmitted in any form or by any means—for example, electronic, photocopy, recording—without the prior written permission of the publisher. The only exception is brief quotations and printed reviews.

ISBN:
Hardbound 9781949598285
Softbound 9781949598292

Cover design by Adrienne Quintana
Edited by Marnae Kelley
Pink Umbrella Books

ACKNOWLEDGEMENTS

This book would not have been possible without the incredible support and dedication of several individuals who believed in me and my story.

First and foremost, I am deeply grateful to Claudette Richmond, who has been by my side for the past three years, meticulously revising and editing my English. Her encouragement and guidance have been invaluable.

I would also like to extend my heartfelt thanks to Marnae Kelley, whose dedication to copy-editing my manuscript brought clarity and precision to my words. Her attention to detail has made a significant impact on the final outcome.

To Rose Secretan, your unwavering encouragement has been a source of strength. Your belief in my ability to share my story kept me going when the journey seemed daunting.

A special thank you to Patrick Sickland, who has been with me from the very beginning. The countless evenings and dinners spent revising my early writings were pivotal moments in shaping this book. Your encouragement to write in English, despite not being my first language, has been a gift that I will forever cherish.

I am also immensely grateful to Adrienne Quintana for her amazing work on the book cover. Your artistry captured the essence of my story in a way that words alone could not.

Finally, to Pink Umbrella, thank you for your support and help in bringing my first book to life. Your belief in my story and your assistance in publishing it have been a dream come true.

To each of you, from the bottom of my heart, thank you.

Supporters of *The Silent Echo of My Childhood*

I am deeply grateful to the generous individuals whose contributions made the publication of my book possible. Your belief in my story and your support have been instrumental in bringing this project to life through financial contributions. You have all played a crucial role in helping me share my journey with the world. I cannot thank you enough for your kindness and dedication to this cause. I want to extend my heartfelt thanks to:

Mark Ludmer
Scott and Susan Keighley
Arlene DeStefano
Patricia Strickland
Courtney Traub
Rosa M. Rosas

PREFACE

Among the peaks and valleys of our existence, moments linger as poignant echoes, some to be cherished and others confronted with a resolute heart. Our voyage, whether bathed in the gentle light of joy or shrouded in the shadows of adversity, unveils profound revelations about the core of our being and our intricate place within the universe. Yet, some moments remain secret, buried under layers of our subconscious. My subconscious dutifully guarded my secrets for a long time, hidden in locked drawers. Then, a wave of tragic events tore open my bag of secrets, forcing me into a relentless pursuit of my memories long buried in the shadows of my past.

Transcribing memories onto paper, guided by the tender dance of ink and parchment, is a profound exercise that breathes life into the most authentic aspects of our souls. It is through this sacred exercise that the self, that ineffable "YOU," is unfurled and empowered to evolve into its destined form.

In the realm of memory, the illustrious Marcel Proust, a luminary of the literary world, stands as a master in summoning forth bygone worlds, weaving them into the present with such vividness that one can almost taste the fragrances, feel the ambiance, and be transported to the very heart of those scenes.

The summer of 2019 would emerge as an epochal chapter of my life that would push me to confront the most profound of challenges. This was the time when I faced the abyss of losing my cherished partner, Dan—an experience that left me in fragments, grappling with grief.

My heart was in a moaning agony. I started to write my pain. This gesture of taking a pen and writing on a blank sheet of paper made me vulnerable in a unique way. The daily writing began my search for myself, my life, and the significant challenges I faced in childhood. From that moment, I began to uncover the true meaning of my life. I reflected on the mistakes I had made—misplaced priorities and the times I failed to give enough attention to daughter, family, and friends. His death was a stark reminder that life is fleeting, and no amount of wealth, career success, or achievements can replace the love of family and the importance of sharing precious moments with those who matter most. Though it brought many regrets, it also inspired me to make changes and correct the trajectory of my life since he filled my life with happiness. I now find joy in the simplest things, whether it's watching a sunset or regularly reaching out to those I love. Knowing how quickly time passes, I make it a point to send a quick text like "I love you" or "Have a great day"—small gestures that mean everything.

The loss of my husband triggered the loneliness and abandonment issues of my childhood experience. I thought I would never have to relive it again. At the same time, it allowed me to focus on recovery, rebuilding my strength, and deepening my daily life experience. I had to make choices. Live or die. Writing became my daily catharsis and helped my recovery. It was a turning point that made me realize I had a life ahead of me and wanted to live again.

Dan's passing brought me back to my unresolved childhood, filled with wounds and traumas.

In my early childhood, I had many great moments of joy and laughter. These magical moments offered glimpses of my innocence and the happiness I had once known. Unfortunately, tragic circumstances overshadowed the good memories. My parents separated when I was nine years old. Not long after, doctors diagnosed my mother with a rare bone disease. She ended up in a nursing home. At thirteen years old, my life was turned over to the guardianship of the Quebec Government. I was young, confused, traumatized, and abandoned. I was among the forsaken children left in youth prisons where solitary confinement was common practice. It left scars on all of us who were locked up in these horrible establishments where there was no trace of humanity.

Writing allowed me to give voice to my pain. It validated my own experiences and allowed me to reclaim my power and strength. While the road to recovery was arduous, my passion for different forms of art became my compass, guiding me through the labyrinth of wounds and traumas.

My childhood abuse in the foster care system and survival of many tough challenges shaped me. Each phase of my life became a step forward, a declaration that I would no longer allow the past to define me.

Finally, after four years of grieving, my newfound courage replaced my darkest period. Ultimately, I emerged from all my painful experiences. For most of my life, I was immersed in my career, shielding myself from my emotions. Even though I wanted to write, it felt like I had nothing to say—until I allowed my emotions to flow freely, embracing a newfound vulnerability that was essential for my writing. My writing became a beacon of hope and survival. Yet, within this crucible of pain, I have grown, emerging fortified, mightier than ever before. It is my aspiration that the lessons forged in the fires of my experience might offer sustenance to those who tread their own path of survival.

As the memories pour out onto the pages of my story, I aim to inspire the ones who have suffered in silence. I hope this book will help you find your own path to healing. Our wounds may have run deep, but with time, patience, and the courage to face our past, we can reclaim our lives and find the power of our own narratives.

Within the following pages, my journey unfolds. It is a journey marked by loss, shaped by the contours of childhood adversity, and ultimately defined by resilience and renewal. After traversing the abyss, I find myself at the precipice of possibility, my heart brimming with newfound courage. May my words resonate, a testament to the indomitable spirit that dwells within us all.

I dedicate this book to my wonderful husband Dan, whose memories are with me daily; my wonderful daughter Melanie, my daily sunshine; my stepchildren, Courtney (her spouse Emily) and Alex (his spouse Aubrey); and all my grandchildren; also for those whom I loved, with whom I shared laughs and sadness, and those who are not among us anymore.

Lastly, I offer this memoir as a tribute to the souls of the past, particularly those forgotten children whose lives were marred by the cruelties of institutions resembling prisons during the late fifties and sixties in Canada. The scars they bore etched themselves upon my heart, as they did upon the hearts of countless children and teenagers who endured a similar plight. This work stands as a witness of their resilience and a call for remembrance so that history may never again repeat this dark chapter.

CHAPTER ONE

Ravenna, Italy, 2017

"Darling, look what Eduardo drew in my coffee? Beautiful musical notes!" I smiled at Dan.

"Look at mine, sweetie," replied Dan. "They created a pine tree on top." He paused and looked at me, saying with the sweetest voice, "I just love having breakfast in Italy with you, my sweet love!" We savored the joyous ritual that had been part of our marriage since day one—Dan bringing me coffee in bed every morning and often my breakfast during the week. The morning aroma of coffee permeating the air was always a precious moment of my day. Dan continued cheerfully with his theatrical voice, "A coffee in Italy is more than a unique experience; it is a delight!"

We arrived in Ravenna after a romantic trip to Rome, which served as a prelude to the beginning of my mosaic class. We made our way to Ravenna from Rome's Termini station by train. We both adored traveling via the sophisticated Rail Europe TGV, as it allowed us to see the scenic rural regions of Italy in comfortable seats. It was the best way to experience the breathtaking beauty of Tuscany.

Sylvie Larivière-Traub

"It's time to go to my class. Let's go, Dan!" As we prepared to leave, I loudly thanked our barista in my best Italian, "Mille Grazia! Ciao!" and added in English, "Your cappuccino was absolutely amazing!" We left the Palazzo Bezzi Hotel and strolled the beautiful streets surrounded by Renaissance buildings. The hotel was about a ten-minute walk from Luciana Notturni's mosaic studio.

"Sweetie," —this was his favorite term of endearment— "I'm so thrilled to be with you in Ravenna and witness one of your dreams coming true." Dan's support had always been such a big part of my life with him.

"Today marks our first day in Ravenna," I said in a theatrical tone. We spoke that way to each other often. "This is where we will meet one of the world's masters of mosaic art!" My heart raced in anticipation. "Isn't it great being here?" So began my week-long journey to study this ancient art form under Luciana's guidance.

Looking back, I ponder the windy road that led me to Italy. From a tender age, my passion for various art forms bloomed within me. During our first visit to Italy in 2016, I stumbled upon the enchanting world of mosaic art. It was a revelation that left an indelible mark on my soul. The allure of this ancient craft captivated me. It ignited a relentless desire to explore and master diverse artistic expressions. Each new form of art I experienced was a soothing balm for the unspoken pain from the echoes of my childhood. I stood amazed by the magnificent mosaic floors at the ruins in Rome, and the captivating artwork on display at the Rome Capitoline Museum and other archaeological sites. I discovered mosaic art and was stunned by the mosaicist of the Roman Empire, whose work had endured for over two millennia. This was when I found a new passion for this art form. Upon our return from that trip, I confided in Dan and expressed my desire to study this ancient art form that had withstood the test of time for over 2,000 years.

I told Dan that Luciana of the Scuola di Mosaica of Ravenna was widely recognized as one of the most significant mosaic artists in the world. She was an esteemed Master, commissioned by various countries for her exceptional mosaic work, which included a stunning piece created for the New York Police Department. It featured Santa Barbara holding the Empire State Building. I wanted to be able to attend one of her masterclasses.

Dan always supported my new passions, even if some were expensive. Many years before, I had studied interior design and frequently spent money on new furniture or treasures in estate sales.

He once teased me after I returned with an ancient mirror, saying, "Maybe you should take culinary lessons instead!"

We both laughed, and I said, "Did you mean it would be cheaper?" Playfully, I added, "Consider yourself lucky to have found me, as you know there's only one person like me every century."

Dan responded with a tender kiss, "Yes, I am very lucky." Looking back in time, I feel lucky to remember these precious moments we enjoyed together.

Dan loved my passion for the arts. When there was anything I wanted to experience, he usually joined me. I was determined to pursue my dream. Once again, we decided to travel to Ravenna together. While I delved into the study of mosaic art under Luciana's tutelage, Dan would explore the Ravenna Museum and the city. Eagerly, I registered for the class and made the necessary travel reservations. But the road to Ravenna was not a smooth one.

Soon after making our plans, in spring 2017, Dan had a routine physical check-up. A few days after his lab work was done, we received a phone call from the doctor, asking us to come the following day for an appointment. It was unusual, but nothing could prepare us for the devastating news. Cancer. We were in shock, but Dan was ready to fight it.

Sadly, we canceled our journey to Ravenna and took a detour into the land of cancer. We feared the unknown but resolved to beat it. After months of challenging treatments, amidst the rollercoaster of emotions, we received a glimmer of hope. Dan's cancer was in remission. It felt like a miracle, and with grateful hearts, we rescheduled our trip to Ravenna for October of the same year.

Sylvie Larivière-Traub

Finally in Ravenna, our excitement was palpable. It seemed our cancer journey gave us new eyes to see and new hearts to feel.

Dan couldn't contain his amazement as we stood before the school entrance. "Oh! Incredible! Look at these breathtaking ancient mosaics, Sylvie!" The walls were covered with masterpieces and created an awe-inspiring ambiance.

I laughed and gently corrected him, "These works are not ancient but replicas crafted with stone and Byzantine glass, some featuring twenty-two karat gold accents. I feel privileged to use the same materials for the mosaic art piece I will create this week." I gently took Dan's hand, looked at him, and kissed him on the cheek. "Thank you for accompanying me on this journey and sharing in the experience of this master class. It means so much to me."

As we gathered with seven other students eagerly waiting in anticipation, we scanned the unique mosaic pieces adorning the walls. Suddenly, the room grew hushed as approaching footsteps echoed from the back. Our attention turned to the entrance as Luciana gracefully entered, extending a warm greeting. *Benvenuti a Ravenna Scoela di Mosaica,*" she welcomed us with her loud and playful tone.

We introduced ourselves to Luciana with a hearty "Buongiorno" and a sprinkling of basic Italian phrases we practiced while walking here. The room brimmed with excitement as we shared our enthusiasm and poor linguistic attempts. Luciana appeared to be in her early sixties and exuded youthful energy, embodying the expressive and vibrant Italian spirit. Naturally boisterous and animated, I always felt at home in Italy.

Over the week, I came to know Luciana more intimately. Despite her immense talent and accomplishments, she remained humble, modest, and true to herself. She carried a deep-rooted passion for her craft. From a young age, she had garnered acclaim as one of the world's foremost mosaicists. She was revered for her meticulous restoration work on the magnificent ceilings of renowned churches such as St. Mark's in Venice and the Vatican's prized mosaics. Her artistic prowess regularly earned her commissions for grand-scale mosaic pieces. Although universities are free in Italy, only a few can attend the art and restoration studies. Teachers identify talents and refer students to the right schools and universities from a young age.

I pinched myself in disbelief, overwhelmed by the privilege of learning from such a renowned artist. "This week is going to be extraordinary," I exclaimed to Dan, my excitement bubbling. Turning to Luciana, I asked her if Dan could attend some parts of the class. She smiled and, with a joyful tone, loudly replied, "Sì, sì!"

The week I spent with Luciana was incredible. In mosaic art, the traditional method of cutting stone involves using a hammer and a hardie, which is a steel, chisel-shaped bladed embedded in a tree log or a steel base. Cutting the stone into small pieces became a cathartic experience for me. The precise hammer downward strike fractures the material with minimal effort, allowing for greater accuracy. This traditional method became a powerful metaphor for life—the work we must do to shape ourselves into who we are meant to be. Michelangelo once spoke of removing the marble that concealed his subject, revealing its true form beneath. As I meticulously embedded each tessera, the small pieces of stone or glass, I felt the metaphor take shape—not just in the art, but in the ongoing work on myself. The shaping of the glass and stone in mortar was like rewriting my narrative and reinventing myself. However, only the tragedy to soon come would really shape my new self as the individual I was meant to be and start a new journey in my life.

That week spent learning alongside my husband was transformative. Our shared passion for art became a powerful bond, strengthening a connection between us that had begun sixteen years earlier. I thought the feeling would never end. But like all things, this, too, would change.

At the end of the week, we visited the UNESCO Mausoleum at the Basilica of San Vitale, the earliest and best-preserved mosaic monument and most artistically perfect. The exterior, built in the shape of a cross, was made of reused ancient Roman bricks. It contrasted with the interior, where the mosaics covered the vaults and dome walls. The grace and harmony of the mosaics were highlighted by the variety of bright colors: blue, green, gold, and orange. The color blue, interspersed in the form of flowers, stars, and wheels, prevailed over the others and created a solemn and evocative atmosphere, made all the more magical by the light filtering through the alabaster windows. The dome contained the most fascinating part of the decoration. There were nine hundred gold stars against a deep blue sky. This decoration was said to have inspired Cole Porter's song "Night and Day."

At this moment, we approached a tourist and asked her to take a picture of us. "Of course," came the reply, and I handed over the camera. I was flooded with a familiar stomach-stirring vortex of emotions. I know now it was the beginning of the end of us. But I didn't realize it then. The gentleman captured us perfectly, holding each other gently. My body wrapped around his, and my head nestled beside his, oblivious to what lay ahead. We were frozen in time in the depth of our love in a magic city. This photo holds a special place in my heart. It is on my phone's home screen, and I love this special moment locked in the timeline of my life.

Dan's illness cast uncertainty over our lives, yet our time in Ravenna brought immense joy against this daunting backdrop. His condition forced me to confront life and the true significance of art for human beings—a revelation that had eluded me until then. During that week in Ravenna, my husband, a gifted artist himself, was an invaluable companion.

I realized in Ravenna that art was always an outlet and a voice for my emotions from my childhood to now. Like the layers of sediment in ancient stones, my experiences, good or bad, shaped my life story. Each stone I cut and lay side by side was a symbolic act of rewriting, a tangible expression of my personal story. Through art, I found solace, a means to transcend the tragedies of my past. Art was a therapy, but it was only later that I could face the haunting remnants of a childhood marked by destiny's cruel hand, and a hidden burden—my bag of secrets.

CHAPTER TWO

My Love Story – Looking Back

In 2001, a profound change reshaped the trajectory of my life as I left behind my home country of Canada to establish roots in California. The decision was influenced by the aftermath of September 11th, 2001. During that time, I was a partner with a company that focused on developing cutting-edge facial recognition software for law enforcement. Our technology helped apprehend criminals, and we knew it could significantly contribute to the global fight against terrorism.

An intriguing anecdote often surfaces in my memory serving as a poignant reminder of the role of good fortune throughout my life. This streak of unusual circumstances commenced when I was young, consistently guiding me away from perilous situations, whether it was from drowning or fire. Once again, this fortune proved providential when I spontaneously decided to cancel a visit to the World Trade Center on September 11th. I felt mixed emotions about going to New York that Friday. While I usually prioritized important meetings, I chose to cancel the one scheduled for that fateful morning. Having traveled all summer for business, I was exhausted from jet lag. Little did I realize that this seemingly ordinary choice would save my life as the tragic events of that day unfolded. I can't help but feel gratitude for that last-minute decision. It was as if some invisible force had guided me away from danger. I had the strange conviction that my life was saved for an unknown reason.

My move to California was intended as a one-way ticket to the sunny state. I rented a small furnished apartment initially. I felt very lonely, away from my French Canadian roots and friends. However, my daughter Melanie joined me a short time later. Her outstanding skill at developing business relationships with law enforcement officials led her to join me in California to work in our American office. Her presence brought me a lot of joy and happiness.

Destiny led Dan into my life in the same year. It marked a significant turning point in my life. What started as a friendship evolved into a profound and deep-rooted love. We had a unique connection; our conversations were often centered around our shared passion for art.

Dan's loyalty, fun-loving nature, and unique spirit endeared him to me, and I tumbled headfirst into love. The following year, we were married. Our marriage felt like a grand celebration, a harmonious and loving union that fulfilled the need for happiness and for a family I had looked for since my childhood.

One of our profound passions was music. In his twenties, Dan's friends and fellow musicians nurtured his ambitions of hitting the big time in the music industry. His affinity for playing the guitar was truly inspiring. His band loved to engage in spirited jam sessions and did to the very end. Our first two years of marriage, I eagerly joined in these sessions, fearlessly contributing background vocals in a rented Hollywood studio. Despite my admittedly modest vocal abilities, this invaluable time spent together served to fortify and enhance the already strong bond between us.

During his youthful days, Dan's creative flair extended to the culinary sphere as he crafted a medley of vegan recipes. The flavors he created became a sensation among celebrities frequenting Follow Your Heart in the early '70s, an era when the beats of music and heartbeat of veganism thrived together in California. Nestled near the iconic Laurel Canyon, the store attracted a mosaic of legendary artists from the '60s and '70s. Laurel Canyon was the cradle of counterculture activity and attitudes during that era, becoming famous as home to many of L.A.'s rock musicians, such as Cass Elliot of the Mamas & the Papas, Joni Mitchell, Frank Zappa, Jim Morrison of The Doors, Carole King, Brian Wilson of The Beach Boys, James Taylor, and many others.

Dan was in the middle of the music scene and the new vegan era. So many celebrities were going to the store. One time, Michael Jackson showed up and asked for Dan. He had just completed his Victory Tour and wanted to ask for a special favor. He was told that Dan was the best and the only chef in Los Angeles capable of baking great vegan cakes. So, he asked Dan to create his no-sugar and no-flour cake for the Victory Tour party. Some recipes Dan created followed him, and I am always proud to see some of his original recipes from Follow Your Heart in the fresh counters of Whole Foods Market.

While Dan immersed himself in the world of culinary creation, his music didn't miss a beat. At that time, he formed a band, Lift-Off, echoing the steps of iconic artists before him. He was very creative, and in one of his concerts in Santa Barbara Bowl, they had a giant screen showing a lift-off of the NASA shuttle while Timothy Leary was introducing the band. Capital Records acknowledged his talents, but the offer meant parting ways with his bandmates. Dan was a loyal and highly trustworthy person, which precluded any possibility of him having a contract with the giant company. Instead, he chose his friends, which was a testament to the kind of person he was. Looking back to our life together, I will never know if he had any regrets.

He opted for a more difficult path from Los Angeles to Seattle. He had great opportunities over there opening a show for Soundgarden. However, the music scene in Seattle never accepted Dan because Los Angeles transplants were considered far away from the Seattle grunge music.

Daniel was loyal and fun to be with, and it was easy to fall for him. Music, acting, and writing were Dan's lifeblood. His passions and enthusiasm formed the connective tissue of our story in 2001 when our paths intertwined. In 2005, we founded a documentary film production company, embarking on creative projects that infused our lives with joy and a great sense of fulfillment. I had never experienced such happiness. Each artistic endeavor was a brushstroke that painted more excitement onto our shared canvas. Meeting him was like discovering a new spectrum of happiness I'd never encountered before.

This new page in my life established a rock-solid emotional foundation for me. Dan became a devoted husband and a remarkable stepfather to my daughter. He was quite handsome with striking features—thick, wavy black hair, captivating blue eyes, and distinctive eyebrows inherited from his Latvian ancestors. To me, Dan seemed like a gift from the heavens. His smile radiated warmth, and his voice had the power to soothe and reassure me in challenging times.

When I was upset, he often said, "Sweetie, don't worry about tomorrow, just put one foot in front of the other, and everything will be okay." Sometimes he would go further, adding, "You know, Sylvie, you can start your day all over at any time, so there are never any bad days." With him, I learned to reset the button of my day and change the outcome.

In 2017, fifteen years after we pronounced our vows, my life had more to unveil, and tragedy would soon cast a shadow on our happiness. The fight against cancer became our unforeseen adversary, and our lives were about to face a new chapter filled with challenges that tested our love and strength in ways we never imagined.

CHAPTER THREE

A Heartbreak Journey

The memory of that cancer diagnosis still lingers. I had urged Dan to see the doctor, despite his reluctance. We both believed that youth was synonymous with invincibility. Dan's cancer diagnosis led to a cascade of events that rocked our world.

We were unaware of the earth-shattering news awaiting us. Sitting in the doctor's office, anxiety thick in the air, we waited for the news. And then came the words, heavy with their weight: "I'm deeply saddened to inform you that you have stage four cancer." The floor seemed to fall away beneath us. We exchanged glances, with a mixture of shock and distress. The doctor's voice broke the silence, "We estimate you probably have three months." Tears welled up in all our eyes as she shared this heartbreaking prognosis.

As we left the doctor's office, reality began to settle in. Driving home, the world outside felt like a blur. How could this be happening? "Three months?" Dan's voice was a mix of disbelief and despair.

In that moment, I found strength to say, "We must stay strong, no matter how hard it gets."

The days that followed were a haze of shock. We sat on the sofa, trying to grasp the magnitude of the diagnosis. We had already weathered so many losses: my parents, Dan's father, my brothers, and Dan's mother. Yet, the news of Dan's cancer felt like an additional crushing blow. The day after, we canceled our trip to Ravenna and thought it would never happen.

We refused to accept the dire prognosis. We didn't deny the fact Dan had cancer; we defied it. Defiance became our ally, a source of strength that carried us through those initial days. We fought fiercely every day, every hour, every minute, seeking second and third opinions, exploring treatment options, and clinging to the hope of survival.

The cancer conundrum had brought us to our knees, but we rose stronger. We found hope in the darkest moments and cherished every fleeting second. The mosaic of our journey created a portrait of courage, reminding us that while life may break us, it's our response that defines us.

Dan's strength shone through; he pursued treatment hoping for a miracle and faced each challenge with determination, ready to defy the odds. After a few months of treatments, his condition improved, leading to partial remission. It was a glimmer of hope and relief for both of us.

Dan's prognosis of three months extended to seven months. Dr. Hendafar, Dan's oncologist, rarely smiled and was not talkative, just direct to the point. But this time he announced to us with a very rare joyful tone, "Your good condition prior to this helped you fight. I am so happy for you two that you got well."

Dan looked at him skeptically. "Does it mean that I am totally healed? Do you think it could come back?"

Dr. Hendafar did not answer his question. Instead, he solemnly looked at him. "Live in the moment and do what you desire, like traveling—go wherever you want."

Throughout Dan's cancer journey, our life together was bittersweet, shadowed by uncertainty and the knowledge that remission might not last. Yet, his resilience and our love propelled us to cherish each moment, focusing on the present and embracing our doctor's advice.

Back home, I asked Dan, "Do you remember when we talked about traveling the world?"

He replied, "Yeah . . . I always thought we'd have more time."

I chirped, "Let's make the most of the time we have now, Dan. Let's create as many new memories as we can." Urgency fueled us as we rushed to visit as many destinations as possible while his strength allowed. These experiences birthed unforgettable memories, enriched our bond, and let us share the world's beauty. We went back to Italy, enjoying Rome, Tuscany, and the romantic beauty of Venice. Two of my most beautiful memories of Italy were the ride in a Gondola in Venice and a moment captured in a picture in front of the Trevi Fountain in Rome.

We also traveled the United States, embarking on creative adventures closer to home. One of our visits was Memphis, Tennessee. We visited Elvis Presley's hometown and drove through the streets where he grew up. With his spontaneous spirit, Dan captured these moments on film rather daringly. He exclaimed, "Stop the car!" and jumped onto its roof, using it as a camera dolly. Although I was concerned about safety, his enthusiasm and determination amidst the bumpy streets and potholes made the experience quite amusing. Dan's adventurous spirit pushed him to create unique shots despite the risks, and I can't help but smile when I think of that day.

In 2019, Dan's battle took a turn for the worse. The cancer returned with a vengeance, testing Dan's resilience and my resolve.

Dan described his reaction to the news in just a few words. "I thought we had beat it . . ."

I continued encouraging him: "We've faced setbacks before, but we won't give up." The outlook was grim. The cancer had brought us to our knees, but we got stronger.

CHAPTER FOUR

Can I Get More Time?

As his condition declined, our days blurred into hospital stays, battling the relentless onslaught of tumors in his liver and pancreas. Each month brought new hurdles—procedures to open obstructed biliary ducts and the introduction of intravenous nutrition as Dan's ability to feed himself dwindled. The specter of mortality loomed as he relied on IV sustenance. But even in the face of the shadows closing in, his spirit remained unyielding, a fighter unwilling to surrender.

The medical professionals reached a grim consensus—recovery was a distant hope. An unexpected lifeline emerged. Our friend Jim, a marine, suggested the use of total parenteral nutrition (TPN), having seen it bolster badly injured marines.

Advocating for Dan's well-being, I pushed for the TPN, an IV-delivered nutrient-rich meal. Doctors were surprised I knew about it. Skepticism greeted my request, and they deemed TPN futile for a man at death's doorstep. Yet, fueled by hope and determination, we defied their skepticism.

I became a constant presence at the hospital, sleeping on a cot beside him, my unwavering support and encouragement steady. "Miracles can happen," I reminded him, a mantra that slowly rekindled his morale. The medical team also became a regular fixture with their daily visits reflecting the gravity of Dan's condition.

Then came a pivotal morning—Dan awoke with newfound determination, querying the medical team about potential avenues for his recovery. I vividly recall that moment, his question hanging heavy in the air: "Is there anything else you can do for me?" A unanimous consensus emerged: there remained no further interventions to attempt. The team departed, leaving a palpable emptiness in their wake. It was obvious the care team was convinced the hospital would be the last home for Dan.

But then, in a stunning turn of events, Dan miraculously sprang from his bed, and an unanticipated vigor propelled him. His actions left me astounded. He ran out of the room and pursued the medical team in the hallway. Their perplexed expressions were a testament to their disbelief at witnessing a man on the precipice of death summoning the strength to chase after them.

Dan's determination reignited discussions of treatment. Radiotherapy emerged as a possibility to shrink the tumors. With a resolute "Let's do it," he embarked on the next chapter, defying the odds.

A poignant anecdote from that time centers on pizza—our cafeteria's renowned delight. Dan's simple request for a slice amidst his health battle symbolized his spirit. As he savored each bite, his strength seemed to surge like he had tapped into a wellspring of vitality.

A week later, Dan and I returned home with a prescription for TPN and two months of bi-weekly appointments for radiotherapy. The treatments sparked a rejuvenation, granting us more time together.

Amid the fight against cancer, I learned that the medical system does not always aim at prolonging life. However, our care team did everything to give us more time. Radiotherapy reduced the tumors and allowed him to start eating normal foods again.

The calendar of his remarkable recovery marked March 2019, and as the days unfolded, the infusion of TPN into Dan's bloodstream wrought a remarkable transformation. Energized anew, he found strength in composing music and determination to create despite adversity. He also started a collection of vinyls with a new turn table. During spring and summer, we listened and danced to Frank Sinatra's music. He was more romantic than ever. When I am sad about those days, I close my eyes and think of those frozen moments in time, and I can smile again at this memory of dancing to the music in a way I had never danced before.

Dan's musician friends orchestrated weekly gatherings in a studio for a symphony of camaraderie and shared passion. Amid melodies and harmonies, Dan found solace and strength, his fingers dancing across instruments and his voice reverberating with vitality. His friend Mark documented those sessions, capturing moments that resonated with the heartbeat of his rejuvenation.

Bolstered by this resurgence, we embarked on an audacious endeavor—a trip to Hawaii in June. With a fervent desire to experience Pearl Harbor, Dan braved the journey.

During our first week in Honolulu, we explored the historic site under the sun's unforgiving embrace, traversing miles without faltering. The specter of cancer momentarily receded, replaced by the illusion of a world where its shadow ceased to loom. A serendipitous encounter with a Hawaiian jeweler led to an unexpected delight—pearls concealed within oysters. I pried open two, unveiling two pink gems of nature's artistry. Dan insisted I choose a ring, a token of his affection to accompany the lustrous gem.

As the sun set on our idyllic week, reality resurfaced as cancer reasserted its grip. The march of time heralded the return journey, a farewell to Honolulu as we set our sights on Kona. The malignancy, unrelenting, reclaimed its dominance as we grappled with the inescapable.

Sylvie Larivière-Traub

June unfolded with our Hawaiian odyssey, but with our return came a grim proclamation—Dan's lifeline, his chemotherapy, needed to resume. Amidst the sweltering heat of that month, doctors delivered a devastating verdict: six months, at best, remained.

The weight of the news was again crushing, yet Dan's spirit remained unbroken. Music flowed from him in poignant and cathartic compositions. A dream of a video production venture began to take shape. Amid this tumult, I stood by him, an unwavering pillar of support, reflecting his determination to extract every iota of life from the time remaining.

The battle raged through July and into August, a month that marked the beginning of his reliance on a walker. As we returned to the hospital, a sense of homecoming mingled with the stark realization that this was where his final days would unfold.

CHAPTER FIVE

The Last Homecoming

During the stifling heat of late June to mid-August, the hospital became a second home for Dan. The sterile walls and antiseptic scent felt like unwelcome guests. Each passing day brought a new onslaught of bad news delivered with a heavy silence. The sun, usually a beacon of warmth and vitality, now seemed to mock him as it filtered through the curtains, casting shadows on his pale, worn face.

And through it all, Dan and I clung to faith and steadfast hope for a miracle. We anchored ourselves to the memory of the months prior, when resilience had pulled him from the brink, refusing to let despair get the best of us. Family and friends stood by his side, their eyes mirroring his own fear and uncertainty. Their unspoken support was the only anchor holding him to the fleeting notion of normalcy.

Up until this point, the dedication of the medical team had been the only force keeping Dan's fragile thread of life intact. Their skilled hands repeatedly inserted stents into his liver to combat the relentless growth of tumors obstructing his biliary ducts each passing month. It had become a routine, a crucial part of the treatment plan established by the doctors following his astonishing recovery in February. While radiotherapy had provided some respite, sustaining him for a brief period with the assistance of the TPN, the relentless progression of the disease now surpassed the limits of our scientific understanding. Despite my encouragement over the past two years, a sobering realization was dawning upon me. The tumors had grown to an unprecedented size, casting a shadow of inevitability over Dan's precarious existence.

The hospital social worker's words echoed in my ears—Dan would be better off at home with his family. So, on August 19th, he returned home by ambulance. His frail body bore the marks of the difficult journey.

We owned a beach cottage in Oxnard Shores. It was to be our dream retirement haven, but now it bore witness to a heart-wrenching reality. I had transformed the living room into a bedroom, anticipating Dan's homecoming for hospice care. Palliative measures were all that remained. The doctors had given us timelines—six months, then two, and now just a week or two.

The hospital had persuaded me to bring him home, but doubt gnawed at me. Would he have been better off in their care? His weakening body had faced too much during transport. But here he was, home, surrounded by family and loved ones. His son, daughter-in-law, and grandchildren gathered, knowing this might be their last meeting. As the day wore on, Dan's strength continued to wane. For the first time, he struggled to swallow, a bad omen. I watched as he drifted into sleep, almost like a coma. The living room buzzed with tension and love, a bittersweet atmosphere that hung heavy. Eventually, everyone left, leaving Carolyn, our friend, and a caregiver by our side.

The night arrived, cold and cruel. My husband was slipping away, his condition worsened by the minute. Exhausted and emotionally drained, I fell into a fitful sleep. Around three in the morning, Carolyn woke me up. Dan was asking for me. Rushing to his side, I found him in a deep sleep again. Little did I know he would never wake again.

His breathing became labored, and I called the nurse in a panic. Following her instructions, I administered the prescribed morphine and a pill. Dan seemed peaceful, breathing slowly. But in the span of a heartbeat, he stopped breathing altogether. Panic consumed me. I cried out to Carolyn and the caregiver, "He's gone! Please help me. He's gone!" I called the nurse again, sobbing, feeling responsible for his passing.

Morning broke, and with it, the harsh reality. Dan's face was emaciated, his body very still. He was fifty-eight years old but looked eighty. Cancer had ravaged and consumed his whole body. My heart ached as I looked upon him, the love of my life, forever stilled. The man who had fought valiantly against cancer had finally succumbed. Guilt and grief washed over me as I realized I had slept a few hours instead of being with him every minute of his last time with me.

The sunrise heralded the end of an era, the end of our life together. My husband, my love, was gone. The pain was overwhelming, a knife to my heart. Half of me had died with him, leaving an immense void.

Every moment without him was a reminder of the vibrant life we had shared. The beach cottage felt desolate, the ocean's beauty tainted by absence. He had been my joy, my laughter, my companion. His smile, forever etched in my memory, would never grace this earth again. I whispered through my tears, "I will miss you, my Dan, every day for the rest of my life. You will never be able to see what I see, to feel the sun on your skin, to feel the breeze in your hair, to smell the fragrance of the ocean, to share the beauty in all things, to laugh with me, and to make me laugh. I will never again see your beautiful smile."

My soul mate was gone, leaving a chasm in my life. My daughter and I had lost the family we had found in Dan and his loved ones. The happiness we had finally known was snatched away.

Dan's journey was over, leaving me to navigate this new reality alone. And so, I faced the future without him, trying to carry his presence in my heart as I entered the tunnel of despair.

The happiness that had come into my life and now had been taken away, again. There was a black hole in my chest, a tunnel of despair with the feeling of neglect, loneliness, and emotional distress from the past. The silent echoes of my childhood distress attacked me full force. I was left behind, abandoned, again.

CHAPTER SIX

The Profound Impact of Love and Loss

"Ever has it been that love knows not its own depth until the hour of separation."
– Kahlil Gibran

Love's depth becomes apparent in moments of separation or loss. These instances illuminate the significance of the roles our loved ones play and the emotional bonds we share. In the comfort of love, it's easy to overlook their presence. Yet, it's the wrenching moments—distance, time, or death—that truly reveal the depth of our emotions. These moments evoke longing, emptiness, and profound sadness. Losing my soul mate, my love, my confidant, and my partner in crime has left me with overwhelming sorrow. In Dan's absence, I now understand the true worth of our connection.

Love transcends time and space. It's through separation or loss that I fully experience the force of this emotion. I'm discovering the importance of treasuring connections and recognizing the enduring love that enriches my life. While separation is painfully bittersweet, it reminds me to express and value love while it's present. Through these challenges, I'm growing and gaining insights into the profound impact of love.

Sylvie Larivière-Traub

Dan's battle with cancer showed his strength, but on August 19th, 2019, he returned home, weakened. The beach cottage, once happy, became a backdrop for his last days. He was where he was loved, slipping first into a coma, and then, within hours, he was gone.

That day is etched in every cell of my being, with sorrow, with longing, with love, and with gratitude for my time with Dan. Losing Dan was, and sometimes still is, unbearable. He was taken away from me too young, and I longed for more of him. The loss left a void like a piece of me was ripped away. I floundered, wounded and isolated. The grief was undeniable, manifesting in my chest. The pain was real, sharp, and heavy. I fell into depression, struggling with daily tasks.

Dan's passing left me vulnerable, with no defenses, and unlocked the vault of my childhood traumas, leading first to more pain but then to self-discovery. His absence reminded me of the loneliness of my childhood, echoing the abandonment and the feeling of not belonging. I felt like an outsider without Dan. An unfillable void replaced the happiness he had brought.

These deep emotions left me no protection, no way to push down the sadness I denied all my life. Floods of family members who had passed without me processing the impact rushed to my heart, demanding to be grieved. My mother-in-law, Kathy: one of the kindest people I ever met, always happy and smiling. Robert, her husband: an eccentric and wonderful human being with blond hair and blue eyes, tall and of solid stature. As a merchant marine, Robert went around the world from the Arctic to the Antarctic. He later joined the coast guard and roamed the California Channel Islands, keeping boaters safe.

One of the hardest losses was my mother and her cherished old piano. I remembered her long-lasting illness and how she had to abandon me. Through it all, I remembered the love, how she longed for me too. My father was difficult, abandoning me outright. All I could feel was my longing for his love.

The Silent Echo of My Childhood

I loved thinking about my older brother Richard, who played with me, protected me, took me for ice cream, and saved me for so long. Why had he mysteriously let me go to the hellish child prison? Still, all I could remember was his love. I love to think of my time with Richard. My heart still aches as I reflect on his passing, a mere fifteen months after he began his valiant battle with colon cancer.

I could only think of my loved ones who are no longer here. Each met me in the tunnel of grief, calling for resolution and release.

I'd had no time to grieve my in-laws before Dan was diagnosed with cancer. I was in a dark place. I could only think how much I would miss my Dan every day, about how I would never see his beautiful smile and hear his sweet voice.

Dan's memorial service was in September 2019. Before the service, my legs began to shake, my chest became tight, and I could hardly breathe. Then, in desperate sobbing, I fainted and collapsed before his open coffin. Unable to grasp the reality of the moment, unable to breathe, I begged for Dan to come back. I was inconsolable. Friends and my pastor surrounded me, trying unsuccessfully to comfort.

Knowing I had to gather myself, I clung desperately to a phrase I heard from others who journeyed through the grief tunnel: "Through it all, love endures." I whispered it quickly, over and over, a prayer to my soul, wishing myself through the tunnel to the other side. Then, I saw the eyes of others looking down at me, also in their grief. I could feel Dan urging me to console them. So, I did. I stood up to find Dan's friends and family, who were concerned for me. I realized we were together in grief, and I reached out to hug each one. It felt good to reach out. I was no longer alone. I could feel Dan smiling.

At the end of the service and after the food and celebration of Dan's life, I returned to the beach house, and the intense grief overcame me once again. It is a cliché to say that I had a broken heart, but sorrow and grief are physical experiences. I could feel my heart aching like a wounded animal. An extreme emotional pain hit me right in the gut. My body hurt all over. I plunged into a state of shock and sorrow. The sudden pain of my loss stabbed my lungs. For a long time, the void of his death was unbearable. I sobbed for what seemed an eternity.

But finally, the day came when I was out of tears. I knew I needed a reprieve from the incessant pain, so I reached out and asked for help from my daughter and my friends. Interestingly, healing began with writing. I began, first talking to Dan, then just daily journaling, as an outlet. Putting pen to paper, again, and again, and again, writing my soul, writing my pain, writing my past. It helped me confront my trauma as I explored life's meaning and walked bravely to my new destiny.

Separation, though painful, is teaching me to cherish moments and express love as I go. The journey through sadness tests us and leads us to self-discovery and a deeper understanding of life's complexities. The enduring power of love guides me, even when my beloved is no longer with me.

The aftermath of this period of my life would bring out a long-forgotten past hidden in my bag of secrets.

CHAPTER SEVEN

My Bag of Secrets

Losing a loved one often forces us to confront buried emotions and memories. The pain of Dan's passing not only compounded my sense of loss but also unearthed the deep-rooted feelings of abandonment from my childhood. Memories I believed I'd buried for over four decades came flooding back. The wounds and memories I had pushed away for over forty-five years resurfaced.

I recalled the pain of my parents' separation, my mother's deteriorating health, and that heart-wrenching moment she was moved to a nursing home, leaving me adrift in a system of foster homes and institutions. I was angry at my father for being an alcoholic and violent because I could not have a normal life. The serial losses I experienced added to this long-time-forgotten feeling of abandonment from my childhood and teenage years. My brother Richard had filled my emotional needs for years, only to have me whisked away to foster homes and institutions. I was a child, and I didn't know why, so naturally I thought it was my fault and buried the memory in shame. I had repressed these sad memories until then and locked them out. I thought I had lost the combination of this lock forever, but Dan's passing reopened my wound.

A conversation I once had while working at the National Film Board of Canada in the early 1980s encapsulated my struggle to face my past. One day, while I was immersed in a research project, my phone rang. On the other end was a producer from Radio-Quebec, a renowned TV network in Montreal. "Would you be willing to discuss the horrific conditions you experienced in those institutions the Youth Tribunal sent you to? Would you publicly denounce the government for the abuse you endured?" the producer questioned.

From the 1950s until 1972, countless children and teenagers, including myself, faced inhuman treatment in these institutions. Though I was in my twenties at that time, the wounds were still fresh. Like a rape victim, I felt an overwhelming shame that led me to decline the producer's request. Sadly, the documentary never materialized, as many of us weren't ready to share our stories.

Only a select few colleagues knew of my tormented past. They believed sharing my story with Radio-Quebec would bring justice to the suffering children of the sixties. Yet, after that call my narrative remained hidden, a secret I locked away for another forty-five years.

But then, after losing Dan, I found myself grappling with the void he left behind. His family, who had embraced me during holidays and celebrations, was gone, passed to the other side, now only a poignant memory. Alone in California, I felt like an alien on a foreign planet.

The road to recovery was one of the most challenging periods of my life. When I started writing about my story, it was as if I had pushed a red button to release my wounds, memories, and numerous drawers filled with stories.

As I wrote, I discovered a profound sense of liberation. Putting my experiences, thoughts, and emotions into words became a cathartic journey. It allowed me to process and understand my past in ways I never had before. Each sentence I crafted felt like shedding a layer of weight I had been carrying for years. The more I wrote, the more I unraveled the complexities of my identity, finding clarity and peace in the narratives I created. Writing became not just an expression of my inner world but a means of reclaiming my voice. The process freed me from the constraints of silence and the shadows of unspoken memories, ultimately transforming my pain into empowerment and my story into a source of strength and inspiration. The silent echo of my childhood had finally reverberated into words, and my story was not silent anymore.

CHAPTER EIGHT

The Old Piano

My suppressed memories, locked away for so long, suddenly felt vividly present with Dan's departure. Intertwined memories of my mother and husband took me on an emotional journey back to my mother's cherished piano.

When I reflect on my childhood, one memory stands out—the presence of my mother's old piano, which was passed down from my grandmother. My grandmother would get so engrossed in the piano's melodies that she'd forsake her chores. Before I even knew how to form memories, that black wooden piano had claimed a space in my heart.

Its joyous melodies were perfect to my ears. I was enchanted by the black keys elevated above the white and the well-worn music manuscripts poised atop, begging to be played. I'd sit on the piano stool, daydreaming about playing those tunes like my mother did. Statues of Beethoven and Wagner stood beside these manuscripts, guardians of our musical moments. After my mother's passing, these statues were all I had left of her. Yet, fate dealt another blow when these sculptures broke during a move, leaving me clutching their fragments, symbolic of my fractured memories.

The memory of the piano was a portal, wonderfully transporting me back to the times I had with my mother. I'd incessantly ask her to play Beethoven's Moonlight Sonata, my absolute favorite. Enthralled, I'd watch her slender fingers dance over the keys, a sight that felt nothing short of magic to my young self. These memories of us enveloped in the music remain vivid, and even today, they bring tears to my eyes.

Later, the intricate beauty of musical notations inspired me to paint them along with musical instruments when I started oil painting in my early twenties. As I began to play the piano with dreams of mastering Beethoven's Sonata, I realized I could never attain the perfection my mother achieved.

Now it's Melanie, my daughter, who carries the torch of this musical legacy. Her fingers on the keys bring back echoes of my mother, though, tragically, they never shared these moments together. My mother passed away when Melanie was just a toddler.

A poignant episode from the past involved the inevitable sale of that beloved piano. My mother's declining health meant she couldn't keep our home, and she also had to part with the piano. That day signified more than just the loss of a beloved instrument; it marked the beginning of my slow and painful journey of losing her.

CHAPTER NINE

An Idyllic Childhood Shattered in Pieces

My early childhood in the Montreal suburbs was a whirlwind of idyllic moments, akin to a gentle summer breeze. I spent those years surrounded by lush pastures, fields, and meadows, and nature played the role of a perfect backdrop to my unburdened days. Every moment was an embrace from the universe, a world that felt without fault.

In the warmth of our home, I remember the joy of assisting my mother in the kitchen, perched on a chair. She would hand me a spoon to mix the cake batter or guide my hand to stir the Jell-O powder. Oh, how I treasured those times in her presence. Her love and kindness radiated, enveloping me in warmth. She'd tell me my story, that I was born with a smile and would wake up every morning singing songs. My mother is written on my heart in the permanent ink of love.

And then there was my father, who flooded my heart with joy every time he returned from work. I would leap into his arms with uncontainable excitement. Every Friday night, he had a special treat for me—a chocolate bar, a delightful anticipation that colored the day with happiness.

We had a beautiful collie who I loved dearly. He was a loyal and lovable companion who seemed larger than life itself. On summer weekends, my father and I would take walks with Coco. Our strolls often led us to the ice cream shop, where Coco's mischievous side would shine through. Much to my dismay, he had a habit of devouring my ice cream cone. My father would chuckle at the situation, and upon seeing my tears would swiftly buy me a new one, ensuring Coco didn't misbehave. This is one of the most vivid memories of my early childhood. I was probably between no more than two or three years old.

I had two older brothers—Richard and Francois. Richard, the eldest, was ten years ahead of me. Francois, the curious explorer of our family, possessed a passion for rhetoric and storytelling. During dinnertime, he would captivate us with his talented speeches, giving us a glimpse into his creative mind. He loved crafting stories and often shared them with me at bedtime, weaving tales that held me captive with their suspense.

Richard, on the other hand, approached the world with a scientific mindset. He nurtured a love for photography and dreamed of becoming a photojournalist. He documented my childhood with numerous pictures, capturing snapshots of my daily life, my growth, and the laughter that echoed through our days. From the moment I took my first breath, I became his model. I have a vivid picture of him combing my hair, Elvis Presley style, with the widest smile on my face. As his little sister, I followed him everywhere, even from my very first steps.

Richard was my adventure companion. Sometimes he would take me on the river in an old rowboat he had. One fateful day, as a gentle breeze transformed into a gust of wind, our rowboat capsized. I was trapped beneath it without a life jacket, desperately trying to keep my head above water. I cried out for help, and then Richard swam under the rowboat and rescued me. He gripped my arm tightly, guiding us both to the safety of the river's edge. Thankfully, he was a skilled swimmer. It took me many years to gather the courage to venture back into the water, but that day, Richard became my protector, my guardian. If he was by my side, I felt invincible. This incident remained a secret from my parents throughout their lives.

History and archaeology ignited my curiosity from an early age. I would collect scrapbooks dedicated to dinosaurs and archaeological discoveries like Tutankhamun and the treasures unearthed from his tomb. My mother would keep magazines for me filled with pictures that fueled my passion. I dreamed of becoming an archaeologist traveling the world searching for hidden treasures. In my young mind, I envisioned myself as an Indiana Jones-type adventurer. The field surrounding our house became my playground of exploration, a place where I imagined hidden treasures that awaited discovery.

When I was five years old, we moved to Montreal. My mother formed new friendships. One of her new friends was Colette. She was our neighbor and had a son, Nick, who became my constant companion. Both of us were shy and often bullied by tough kids in the neighborhood. Our shared challenges bonded us, and Nick became my best friend. We were inseparable, drawing and painting together, embarking on woodland adventures in search of forgotten treasures. The northern outskirts of Montreal still held patches of woodlands, a haven for our curious souls.

We loved roller skating during the summer, attaching adjustable-size roller blades to our shoe soles with a key. They may have been vintage or old-school, but to us, they were the epitome of joy. Our home was nestled on a corner of a hill street, and we relished the exhilarating thrill of zooming down on our roller skates. In winter, we traded our roller skates for ice skates and spent countless hours at the ice rinks.

I enjoyed my years at school from grade one to seven. It was a catholic school just for girls managed by nuns. The education was very good. We had music and singing classes, history, geography, and the regular classes. Music and history were my favorites.

My mother loved doing watercolors and it was an activity that we both shared. I started classes in visual arts at a young age. Her best friend was the director of the Montreal School of Fine Arts and had a class on Saturday for kids. I started in her class when I was around five or six years old. Painting with my mother and friends was an encouraged activity at home.

Most of my childhood was wonderful, and I believed my world was perfect. By the end of my sixth year, however, that illusion was shattered as I experienced the dark side of my family, a big elephant in the room I had never seen before.

CHAPTER TEN

The Harsh Truth

I turned seven years old on November 9th, 1961, and the idyllic world of my childhood crumbled.

My father, an alcoholic, had a volatile personality when under the influence and became the focus of our lives. Until then, my older brother Richard had shielded me from the fights and protected me from witnessing our father's erratic behavior. However, after we moved to Montreal, Richard, my unwavering protector, began working part-time at the local grocery store and had to leave our home more frequently. During this time, I became a firsthand witness to my father's violent outbursts. In these instances, he would yell at us, his face red, and his eyes became so dark. Scared, I would hide under my parents' bed.

I often wondered why I hadn't seen it before. In later years, Richard confided in me, sharing the secret of how he would whisk me away whenever problems and violence erupted. He would take me outside to play or visit his friends, ensuring that I was spared from witnessing our father's rage.

The truth was hard to accept. I realized my family was far from perfect, and my father's alcoholism and volatile nature were terrifying. Domestic violence, a term not widely recognized in the late fifties and early sixties, plagued my mother. Every night, she would anxiously gaze out the window, awaiting my father's return from work. At the time I didn't understand the reason behind it. Sometimes, she would silently guide me to the back of the house, cautioning me to be quiet as we tiptoed away. It puzzled me because it was often dinnertime.

"Is it the hat, mother?" I asked, knowing she was reading a sign.

"What do you mean?" Mother asked, keeping a keen eye on the window.

"It's his hat!" My mother looked surprised. "I'm right, aren't I? If his Humphrey Bogart hat is askew on his head—it means he's been drinking. That's your cue for us to leave." I looked at her proudly.

"Oh, you are too smart. Let's get to the back room!" She led me down the hallway.

During those years, I witnessed countless instances of my father's violent behavior, and I struggled to comprehend why he acted that way. On Saturday mornings, we would often play card games together, and he would patiently teach me the rules. I cherished those moments, unable to reconcile the sweet and loving father I knew during those sober times with the monstrous transformation alcohol brought forth. My father's alcoholism turned him into a Mr. Hyde.

The first time I witnessed my father's anger in full force was after our move to Montreal. He erupted in a fit of rage, shouting at my brother and hurling a ketchup bottle in his direction. It splattered against the wall, leaving a vibrant red stain. At that moment, my idealized image of my father shattered, replaced by shock and disbelief at his aggression.

It is interesting to reflect on how, years later, I would marry a violent man who exhibited similar behavior, even resorting to throwing food on the wall when displeased. "The sins of the fathers," they say. I recall one incident with my first husband where mustard and relish splattered the walls and kitchen cabinets, leaving behind a pale yellowish tone that persisted, even after cleaning.

Soon after, my nights became plagued with nocturnal terrors, which started the beginning of a dark and troubled chapter in my childhood.

CHAPTER ELEVEN

Nightmares and Night Fears

Every evening when the clock struck eight, my mother would lead me to bed, marking the end of the day. Each night, accompanied by my mother's soothing voice and a gentle goodnight kiss, a sense of unease would settle in, tainting my sleep. With the nighttime ritual came an expectation that darkness would bring forth terrible nightmares.

Drifting into slumber came effortlessly, lulled by the distant hum of my mother's presence in the kitchen. But without fail, around one o'clock in the morning, ghostly nightmares would seize me and thrust me into a realm of terror.

"Mama! Mama, please!" I'd wake up in a cold sweat, trembling, my heart pounding, consumed by an overwhelming sense of dread that clung to me until dawn finally dissipated the darkness.

In the initial weeks of these nightly terrors, I sought solace in my parents' comforting bed. Timidly, I would approach, "Mama, are you awake?" Perceiving the depth of my anxiety, my mother would welcome me to nestle beside her, offering solace in the sanctuary of her loving arms.

However, as time wore on, my father deemed me old enough to remain in my own bed, demanding with hate and anger in his voice, "She's too old for this. Send her back to her bed now!" He added, "It's not normal for a nine-year-old to sleep with the parents."

Soon the nightmares evolved into full-blown night terrors, gripping me with indescribable fear. I felt trapped amidst a spine-chilling horror movie like the one I had seen about a lone babysitter left to confront an unseen intruder in a house. The only tangible aspect of my fears was the relentless anticipation of an imminent attack. Once awake, my sweat was dripping in my face and my head turning frenetically to my left and my right, looking for any intruder who might hide or suddenly appear to hurt me. Everything was in my head, but it seemed so real it was hard to see the difference. Once daylight came early morning, all my fears began dissipating.

Our modest home boasted a lengthy hallway adorned with an exquisite Persian rug. In the middle stood a telephone table with an attached chair. To the left was the bathroom. My parents' bedroom resided on the right, and my brother's room stood across from it. In the turmoil of my nighttime terrors, I sought refuge in the chair by the telephone table and pressed my back against the reassuring wall. From this vantage point, I had the best chance to detect any potential intruders who dared to breach our sanctuary. This position granted me a glimmer of respite from the ceaseless fear that plagued me.

As the years passed, my fear gradually subsided, but it resurfaced sporadically until I reached the age of thirty-eight. It defied reason, yet it clung to me tenaciously, as an unwelcome companion that refused to be cast aside.

Many nights, I sought refuge on the piano bench, positioned near the edge of my mother's bed. For hours I would sit there, finding a semblance of comfort and security. Sometimes, I would remain seated until morning arrived, the proximity to my mother providing a faint glimmer of reassurance.

My lack of sleep began to take its toll. I frequently dozed off at my school desk, desperately struggling to maintain focus. There were instances when my mother, awakened from her slumber, would witness my distress as I sat by the piano. In those moments, she would quietly beckon me to join her on her side of the bed, without waking up my dad. The respite of additional sleep proved invaluable, and as my head rested upon her chest, a sense of tranquility washed over me.

Night after night, the vividness of these nocturnal terrors was so intense that it would catapult me from the safety of my bed, heart pounding, racing to turn on the light in my hallway. Each night felt like a battle against unseen forces that dredged up fears and memories I couldn't fully escape. The darkness became a canvas for my deepest anxieties, painting scenes of dread and despair that left me breathless and disoriented upon waking.

Despite the passage of time and the supposed wisdom that comes with age, I still reacted like a frightened child, seeking solace in the warm glow of a light. It was as if the simple act of illuminating my room could banish the shadows within my mind, providing a reprieve from the haunting cries of my subconscious. These nightly episodes were a stark reminder of unresolved traumas and the persistent grip of my inner demons.

It was only recently that I learned I was suffering from post-traumatic stress disorder (PTSD). I was to live many more traumatic events in my life.

CHAPTER TWELVE

A New Life with My Mother

When my parents separated, I was about ten years old. My mother found a modest apartment to share with me and my two brothers, which started a new chapter in our lives. With a newfound independence, my mother embraced her fresh start as she took her first job. We lived in the vibrant neighborhoods of North Montreal, where she worked hard to make ends meet. My older brother Richard also helped with groceries and other household needs. He made sure I had the clothes I needed.

One day, my mother came home with my uncle, who owned a bicycle shop, with two nice bicycles for me and my mom. My uncle had refurbished the bicycles for us. It was a big surprise, and we enjoyed riding our bicycles in the neighborhood. I took care of cleaning it every week. I was proud to ride my shining bicycle.

We would go riding regularly. Mother's laughter echoed through the streets as we pedaled along. It filled me with a sense of boundless happiness and contentment. I felt as if the world was a place brimming with endless possibilities. Little did I know that those blissful years would soon be overshadowed by tragedy.

During that period, my father lived close to our home. We agreed that I would meet him every Sunday for a special lunch at our favorite restaurant. I cherished those hours spent with him. During that time, he abstained from drinking, which was probably a condition for our Sunday meetings.

"Meet my beautiful daughter. She's as smart as she is pretty!" He would beam with pride as he introduced me to everyone he knew.

His eyes would light up as he spoke about me, and it made me feel incredibly special and loved. Without fail, he would ensure I indulged in my favorite dessert. "A slice of warm pie topped with a generous scoop of ice cream for my beautiful daughter," he would say, smiling from ear to ear. I can still vividly recall those Sunday lunches because they were the moments when my father was at his best—clear-headed and present.

Reflecting on those times, I am grateful to my mother and brothers for shielding me as much as they did from the harsh realities of our circumstances. During those early childhood years, I reveled in innocence, cocooned in love and care. They protected me from the full weight of my father's struggles, which would later become a heavy burden on my shoulders.

Those memories became my sanctuary. They fortified me for the challenges that lay around the corner. In my young eyes, it seemed like I still had a good family, an unbreakable bond forged by love. Little did I know that the strength of that bond would be tested, and the path ahead would be far from easy. I was unaware of the storm brewing on the horizon.

CHAPTER THIRTEEN

A Cold Night

It was a cold November night in Montreal, the kind where the biting chill seemed to seep through your bones. I clutched my mother's hand tightly as we made our way to the grocery store, my breath forming small clouds in the air. Suddenly, without warning, her hand slipped from mine, and she crumpled to the ground with a pained cry. I was only nine years old.

"Mother, are you all right?" I cried, panic rising in my chest as I tried to help her up. Tears welled in my eyes as I desperately tugged at her, my small hands trembling. "Mother, please, you have to get up!"

But as I struggled to lift her, she spoke words that would forever be etched in my memory. "I can't feel my legs." Her voice was laced with fear, and the realization hit me like a tidal wave—she couldn't get up. A man walking toward us came to help her. Once up, my mother said she was feeling better and could walk again.

In the years that followed, my mother's illness became a relentless presence in our lives, slowly unraveling the fabric of our family. Hospital smells, the sterile sights and sounds, and the ever-present pain became all too familiar to me. From the age of nine until I turned thirteen, I lived with my older brother Richard, as my mother's health steadily declined, casting a shadow over our home.

The distress in her eyes as she watched me cry was unbearable. Eventually, she underwent various treatments in an attempt to alleviate her suffering. Cortisone was prescribed—a medication whose side effects were not fully understood at the time. The damage it caused to her joints was devastating, leaving her with a painful combination of bone disease and arthritis.

By 1964, my mother's condition worsened. The bone disease tightened its grip, and surgeries to repair her femur only led to complications. She returned home, but now she was confined to a wheelchair for a while, using a cane intermittently. I remember kneeling beside her and softly saying, "It's okay, Mother, I'll take good care of you." I meant every word, even though the weight of those responsibilities was far beyond my years.

After school, I stepped into the role of caregiver, helping with dinner and managing household chores. I vacuumed, dusted, and did laundry for my mother and brothers, who worked long hours to keep us afloat. My mother, who had once been so vibrant and connected to the world of art, fell into a deep depression. The spark that had defined her was slowly extinguished. A social worker was assigned to accommodate her special needs, and she became a constant presence in our lives, her visits bringing an unsettling sense of foreboding.

After numerous hospitalizations, the doctors finally placed my mother in a rehabilitation hospital for long-term care. Weekends became bittersweet as I boarded the bus to visit her, the love and longing I felt for her growing stronger with each passing day. Yet, there were brief moments when she felt better, managing to walk short distances with a cane. But these glimpses of normalcy were fleeting, and the social worker began quietly advocating for my mother's transition to a permanent nursing home, convinced it was the best course of action.

With each visit, the social worker wove a narrative of care and support, gently persuading my mother that a nursing home would provide the specialized attention she needed. Slowly, the idea took root, and under the advice of the social worker, my mother agreed. I was around twelve years old when she moved permanently into the nursing home, and I stayed with my brother Richard.

This decision marked the beginning of a tumultuous chapter in my life. For the first time, I felt the bitter sting of abandonment, a soul-crushing separation from the person I held dearest. Richard and I were left to grapple with the painful realization that our familiar haven of love and warmth would never be the same. With heavy hearts and tear-stained cheeks, we bid farewell to the life we had known and stepped into an uncertain future, burdened with sorrow and longing.

CHAPTER FOURTEEN

Living with My Brother

After my mother was admitted to an assisted living facility in early 1966, Richard and I continued to reside in the apartment she had rented after separating from my father. I had become skilled at managing our household during my mother's frequent hospitalizations. Despite coming from a broken family, Richard remained my unwavering support, and played the roles of both surrogate father and beloved older brother, providing stability in our familiar environment.

Richard made it a priority to ensure my well-being and made sure I got those chores done. He also provided me with a weekly allowance.

In 1967, Montreal was chosen as the venue for the international universal exposition titled "Man and His World." This grand event featured over eighty pavilions representing various countries and cutting-edge technologies, all inspired by the renowned French pilot Antoine de Saint-Exupéry's book. Among the impressive pavilions, the United States Pavilion stood out with its awe-inspiring design that would later influence the iconic round structure of the Epcot Center. The exhibition's highlight was undoubtedly the captivating display showcasing the future missions of NASA, housed within an enormous biosphere.

Recognizing my excitement for the event, Richard generously purchased a summer passport for me to visit the exposition, granting free entry any day. Utilizing the convenient subway system, I eagerly visited the exposition three to four times a week throughout the summer. The diverse crowd comprised individuals from all corners of the globe. Armed with my passport, I took immense pride in visiting and obtaining stamps from each pavilion. By the end of that remarkable summer, I had managed to explore every single one. On one memorable occasion, Richard accompanied me, and we relished a delightful dinner at the Switzerland Pavilion restaurant, where I indulged in my first taste of delectable cheese fondue.

If it happened to be a weekend, I happily joined Richard on shopping excursions, and he would treat me to meals at restaurants. During his night shifts, which often left me alone during the evenings, I steadfastly waited for his return before retiring to bed. He knew about my fear and nightmares at night, allowed me to keep the light in the hallway, and reduced my night terrors. When I was extremely scared, I would go into his bedroom and sleep in the other bed, previously occupied by my brother Francois.

It was during this period that my brother Francois was frequently hospitalized for schizophrenia. Before my mother went to the assisted living facility, Francois had moved into an apartment and was working at my cousin's company. It was then that he began to show symptoms of what would become a long and debilitating illness, marked by years of suffering. While working at my cousin's company, he started a fire, which, fortunately, was extinguished quickly.

The next ten years were punctuated by hospitalizations, interspersed with periods where he seemed to improve. However, his condition steadily worsened. I remember his phone calls, crying to me about the horrifying hallucinations he would see in his apartment. I remember one of these calls. He was in his bed with hallucinations of snakes all over his bed.

One of the last times he was still living in his small apartment, I visited him. The kitchen was filled with rotten food, and the apartment was in a state of neglect, with food even scattered on the floor. It was clear that he could no longer live on his own. Seeing my brother in such a state was heartbreaking. He was eventually interned in a mental hospital, where he remained for the rest of his life.

The strain on our family was immense. My mother, already frail and unable to care for herself, was heartbroken over Francois' condition. Despite the medications and therapies, his mental state continued to decline. There were moments of lucidity, brief flickers of the brother I once knew, but they were fleeting and increasingly rare. Each visit to the hospital was a painful reminder of the brother I had lost to this terrible illness. The mental hospital became a second home for him, a place where he was safe, yet isolated from the world he once knew. His calls became less frequent over time, his voice more subdued, as if the disease was slowly consuming his spirit.

Looking back, I realize how unprepared we were to handle such a devastating illness. The feeling of helplessness was overwhelming at times as I watched Francois's mind fleeting away. Watching someone you love deteriorate before your eyes is one of the hardest things to witness. The great storyteller he was when I was very young was the only positive thing I could see from my memories.

Sylvie Larivière-Traub

During this period of transition, my mother decided to go permanently into a nursing home. My brother Francois's sickness getting worse month by month was extremely difficult amidst the feeling of abandonment. So, the year of Expo '67 was a great distraction.

One Christmas, at the beginning of Mother's sickness and during one of her hospital stays, one memory stands out vividly among my cherished memories. Richard and I collaborated on creating a beautiful tree adorned with a miniature village. My mother had collected delicate glowing houses that lent a magical ambiance. However, that year there were no gifts beneath the tree. Unfazed by this absence, I creatively repurposed leftover gift wrap and meticulously wrapped towels to create the illusion of presents. When Richard returned from work, he was both intrigued and touched by the sight before him. I confessed that my makeshift gifts were mere towels. The following day, he surprised me with a heartfelt gift—an exquisitely illustrated book chronicling the story of Moses. This precious gift bearing my name on its first page has remained a cherished possession throughout my life and occupies a prominent place on my bookshelf.

I vividly recall the many packaged dinners we shared for effortless meals that required minimal preparation. Since neither of us had really learned to cook with my mother, our meals were extremely simple. I embraced creativity in transforming those simple meals by adding tomatoes, vegetables, and ground beef to provide delightful variations. Chef Boyardee ravioli was one of my favorites. Unfortunately, my culinary skills failed to reach exceptional heights in later years. However, Richard was a decent cook, particularly skilled at preparing steaks on his days off.

Despite the tumultuous circumstances surrounding us at that time, I discovered moments of tranquility and contentment in the presence of my extraordinary older brother.

At the tender age of thirteen, I began venturing out at night with my friends. During this phase of my life, Richard recognized my growing independence and the changes that come with adolescence. He began to worry about my well-being during those solitary evenings. Undoubtedly, his concerns were rooted in the fact that I appeared older than my years, already standing at a height of five feet and nine inches.

My aunts must have become aware of the fact that I spent my nights alone. They deemed it abnormal for a thirteen-year-old teenager to lack evening supervision. And so, the peace I had found in Richard's care was abruptly shattered.

CHAPTER FIFTEEN

Home Hopping

Living with Richard came to an abrupt halt. I was getting into my teenage years and was very precocious. My grandmother recommended to my brother that I go live with her and my aunt for safety reasons. So I would have someone with me at night. Richard now had a girlfriend, the woman he would later marry. It was not easy for him to have a little sister to take care of while trying to navigate his own life.

While I was living with my grandmother, Richard moved into his own apartment. Strangely, he had chosen an apartment with only one bedroom, which left me wondering if I could ever go back to living with him.

I had a close bond with my grandmother. I had spent many lunches with her when going to the primary school that was beside her house. We had a long conversation about her teenage years; she understood, and it was easy for me to follow her guidance.

However, my aunt Alice also lived in the household, and her constant picking on me became a source of distress. I loved her very much and remembered how she spoiled me when I was a little girl. However, as I was going through my rebellious teenage years, growing fast and seeking independence, it became difficult for my unmarried, childless aunt to understand and relate to the complexities of my situation.

Although I wasn't allowed to go out at night, my rebellious nature led me to sneak out, thinking they wouldn't notice. During this time, I began experimenting with drugs, being inspired by the "Peace and Love" movement of San Francisco's Summer of Love in 1968. My unconventional style of dress became a subject of constant discussion and arguments with my grandmother and aunt. It became evident that our coexistence was not feasible.

They decided that I would return to live with my big brother. I soon discovered that this arrangement was only temporary. After a few months, it became too difficult for my grandmother and my aunt to handle a rebellious teenager, and I again found myself in a difficult place. It would be one of the biggest betrayals from my own family.

CHAPTER SIXTEEN

Taken Away

Returning to Richard's new apartment brought a mix of happiness and awkwardness. Since I didn't have my own room, Richard once again selflessly sacrificed his comfort for me by making the sofa his spot. The apartment complex had a swimming pool, and I spent most of my days enjoying the cool waters. In the evenings I went out with friends, but still, there were occasional tensions between Richard and his girlfriend due to my constant presence.

While living with Richard, I transitioned from primary school to high school, entering grade eight. The change was challenging, especially coming from a highly structured Catholic school where I had studied from grades one through seven. Primary school had been tough, not just because of the rigid environment but because I was constantly bullied. Whenever I made a new friend, my tormentors would quickly intervene, warning them that being friends with me would only lead to trouble. As a result, much of my primary school experience was marked by loneliness.

High school, however, was a different experience. The environment was less structured, allowing me to remain more anonymous. I made new friends, and for the first time, I wasn't being bullied. It felt like I was finally starting a new chapter in my life.

One morning, a loud knock on the door jolted me awake. Upon opening it, I found myself face to face with two men dressed in serious gray and black suits. Their intense aura filled me with fear as they introduced themselves. Questions swirled in my mind, but their silence left me bewildered. Suddenly, one of them commanded, "Get dressed. We'll be waiting outside." With no adults present and feeling powerless, I knew I would have no choice but to comply. My thoughts raced. I kept wondering why Richard wasn't there to help and where he could be. Confusion reigned, and the men offered no explanations.

Desperation clawed at the edges of my consciousness as I pleaded for clarity and understanding. The men, their countenances grave and impassive, revealed their true purpose with chilling finality. "We are representatives from the Child Protection Department of the Quebec Government," they intoned, their words laden with ominous portent. In that moment, the illusion of safety shattered, replaced by the harsh reality of government intervention.

"You are now placed under government guardianship," they declared. Their words were a damning verdict that echoed in the hollow chambers of my soul. Yet, little did I know their intentions were far from benevolent. As the facade of protection crumbled, I stood on the precipice of a new reality—one defined by betrayal, uncertainty, and, ultimately, resilience.

Trapped in a suffocating web of circumstances, I reluctantly acquiesced, my mind a tempest of futile escape plans and desperate pleas for reprieve. The confines of Richard's second-floor apartment were devoid of any viable means of fleeing.

As I dressed in my bedroom, the weight of resignation settled heavily upon my shoulders. The oppressive realization of my powerlessness loomed like a specter in the room. Every fiber of my being yearned for escape, for liberation from the shackles of impending doom that bound me.

With trembling hands, I grasped the doorknob, its cold metal a harbinger of the uncertain fate that awaited beyond its threshold.

Every step forward felt like a march toward inevitable captivity, each footfall a solemn echo of resignation. There was no room for hesitation, no space for defiance. As they guided me with unwavering determination, I felt like a lamb being led to slaughter.

Escape became a distant dream, an elusive mirage vanishing into the ether of impossibility. Trapped within the confines of their watchful gaze, I surrendered to the tide of fate, resigned to the chilling reality of my captivity.

The imposing figures escorted me toward a waiting black sedan. Its sleek exterior was a stark contrast to the turmoil raging within me. As the back door swung open, a torrent of tears streamed down my cheeks.

In that harrowing moment, the absence of Richard, my steadfast ally, pierced through the veil of despair, leaving me feeling utterly abandoned.

Questions clamored for attention in the recesses of my mind, demanding answers that remained elusive. Where were they taking me? Why had Richard deserted me in my hour of need? The silence that greeted my desperate pleas only deepened the chasm of despair that threatened to consume me whole.

A flicker of hope ignited inside me with a fleeting red light, flashing a moment of reckless desperation. With trembling hands, I reached for the door handle, my fingers grasping for a glimmer of salvation amidst the suffocating darkness. Yet, the door remained steadfastly locked.

Trapped within the confines of that unyielding car, with no means of breaking free, I surrendered to the inevitability of my circumstances. In that moment of resignation, I felt the weight of my captivity settle upon my shoulders, a heavy burden that threatened to crush my spirit.

As we navigated the familiar streets, tracing the contours of my old neighborhood, a wave of profound longing washed over me. Caught in the current of memories, I found myself at a standstill, gazing out the window at the looming silhouette of my high school.

At the intersection, the significance of that institution became palpable. It was more than just a place of learning; it was a sanctuary of friendship and laughter, a cornerstone of my youth that had shaped the very fabric of my being. Yet, like a fragile dream torn asunder by the harsh light of reality, it had been cruelly snatched away. As the traffic light painted the scene in hues of red and green, a torrent of emotions surged within me, threatening to engulf my fragile composure.

Finally, we arrived at our destination—a four-story building where I would meet my newly assigned social worker. The car parked at the rear, and I was escorted into an office. Glancing around, I couldn't help but notice a sign displaying different department names and their corresponding directions. My heart sank as I read one section: "Youth Tribunal."

CHAPTER SEVENTEEN

A New Beginning in Foster Care

With a mix of apprehension and curiosity, I met with my social worker—a kind-hearted woman in her sixties with short gray hair and glasses. Her warm and friendly demeanor surprised me, easing my initial fears.

She explained that the Martins, a lovely family with eight children of their own, had been chosen as my foster family.

Although the thought of living with such a large family was intimidating, I held onto the hope that I might find some happiness and a sense of belonging.

And so, accompanied by my social worker, I embarked on the journey to my first foster home. The Martins' residence was a small 1930s house with a modest yard, located near a cemetery that lent an eerie atmosphere to the surroundings. Upon our arrival, Mrs. Martin warmly welcomed us into the living room. She was a youthful woman with long, curled red hair and piercing blue eyes. Her husband was still at work, and I would meet him later that night. I discovered that they had a large and friendly German shepherd dog.

After a conversation between my social worker and Mrs. Martin, it was time for me to see my room. Though small, it was impeccably clean. A wooden chair stood near the entrance and a narrow single bed was positioned against the wall. Through the window on the left, I could see the cemetery—a sight that sent shivers down my spine as I spent my first night there.

One of the items I had brought along was my recently acquired guitar, a cheap, student-grade instrument I purchased for a mere five dollars. Despite its limited playability it held sentimental value and adorned my bedroom chair. Though I longed for proper lessons, financial constraints prevented me from pursuing them. Nevertheless, my guitar became a cherished decoration and a source of solace in my new environment. I could strum a few chords, but my skills were limited.

During our initial conversation, Mrs. Martin informed me that I had already been registered at St-Eustache High School where my uniform, a gray skirt, white blouse, and tartan vest, had already been purchased. Classes would start the following Monday. Eager to assert some independence, I decided to slightly shorten my skirt and align it with the trendy miniskirts of that era. However, this deviation from the norm didn't go unnoticed. My teacher promptly sent me to the principal's office to be told that school attire differed from weekend fashion. Consequently, I was sent home to change my skirt. One inch above the knee was the school rule.

It was my eighth grade, and the school was an unexpected, good surprise. I loved the lab class, science, and culinary class.

The foster home I was living in was out of town in a rural area. The girls at school didn't mind the long skirt. It was a different mentality. I loved the school. Everyone was nice. It was a school for girls only. No one was really judgmental about others compared to the primary school I had attended, and there was no bullying. However, at the foster home, I was far from feeling at home.

The Silent Echo of My Childhood

My new life in the foster home was a stark departure from the freedom I had enjoyed in the past year. Adjusting to the structure and routines proved challenging. My curfew prevented me from forming friendships or engaging in extracurricular activities. Mrs. Martin disapproved of me visiting friends in their homes, and I could not invite anyone over. I felt like an outsider—merely residing in a foster home rather than truly belonging to a family.

After school, household chores consumed my time. I was assigned the daily task of floor cleaning and various other duties, as messes were abundant with eight children in the house. I felt I was there as a helper and not under foster care.

Following dinner, I retreated to my room, completed my homework, and spent hours lost in my thoughts. Entertainment was scarce. There was no radio or television to occupy my time. For some reason, I could not enter the living room to watch TV. I think it was reserved only for parents. I struggled to connect with the children in the house and maintained an air of indifference toward my so-called family. It felt as though they were fulfilling their responsibilities primarily to make ends meet while I played the role of a helping hand in raising a brood of children.

Though my life at the foster home wasn't terrible, it was far from being a true home for me. Everything felt foreign, and I experienced an overwhelming sense of abandonment, left to navigate life with only my thoughts for company. The dog often barged into my room and knocked over the chair each time, damaging my guitar. After several falls, the instrument became unplayable beyond the point of repair. Despite its sorry state, I held on to it into my twenties.

On weekends, I had permission to visit my brother Richard. Every Friday after school, I eagerly went to the bus terminal, excited to spend time with him in Montreal. It was a cherished opportunity for me, a chance to escape the confines of my foster home. Although my mother still resided in an assisted living facility, the presence of Richard alone provided me with a sense of relief. However, our weekends together were short-lived because he often worked the night shift on Fridays and Saturdays, which left me to explore the city with friends and return late at night or sometimes in the early morning hours.

One Sunday night, upon returning to my foster home with Richard, I received devastating news from Mrs. Martin: my social worker had decided I could no longer visit my brother every weekend because he was now working weekends. They had learned that he was leaving me alone at night during his shifts. I was heartbroken. Going there on weekends had been a relief because I could go out with my friends. When he had time off, he often took me with him to bars with his girlfriend, Monique. At 5'8" tall, I could easily get in. I suspect that either my aunt Alice or my grandmother heard about this and informed my social worker. Her announcement hit me with a wave of sadness, anger, and betrayal. I rushed to my bedroom and wept for hours.

Though the Martins were kind people, it became evident they didn't truly care about my well-being. I yearned for the presence of my mother, or at the very least my brother. Richard was my family, and now, not even the weekends were mine to spend with him. It felt like being let down all over again. I couldn't help but suspect that it was because Richard, along with my social worker, had discovered my Saturday night escapades in downtown Montreal. With my adult eye, I think he wanted more and more to be free, spending his weekends with his girlfriend. However, the loss of connection with limited visit rights with my family was profound. Nevertheless, I persevered and completed the full school year.

As summer approached, I expressed my dissatisfaction about the limited visits to Richard to my social worker. In response, she made arrangements for me to move to a new foster home in the heart of Montreal so I could visit the weekends he was not working.

The Summer of Love was a social phenomenon during the summer of 1967 when as many as 100,000 people, mostly young people, sported hippie fashions of dress and behavior. The movement centered in San Francisco. More broadly, the Summer

The Silent Echo of My Childhood

of Love encompassed the hippie music, hallucinogenic drugs, anti-war, and free-love scene throughout the West Coast of the United States and as far away as New York City and Canada. Hippies were sometimes called flower children. A few were interested in politics; others were concerned more with art (music, painting, and poetry in particular) or spiritual and meditative practices.

The Beatles and psychedelic experiences became integral parts of my teenage years. Montreal itself was undergoing a cultural revolution, echoing the sentiments of youth-driven protests against the Vietnam War in the United States. In Quebec, we had our own battles against English Canada, proudly waving our distinct flag—the French Fleur de Lys. No other province boasted a different flag; the Canadian Maple Leaf flag was the sole standard. However, this was all before the October Crisis of 1970, when the Front de liberation du Québec (FLQ) kidnapped a few government officials and a minister along with with other individuals. The FLQ terrorists killed the minister. For months, Montreal was under military siege, with an 8 o'clock curfew imposed. It was a sad part of French-Canadian history.

The FLQ included some unidentified members who would later be pardoned and become the founders of the Parti Québécois, which propelled the separatist movement in the 1970s. During the sixties, like the United States, Quebec was in turmoil, undergoing its cultural revolution. It was during these years that I would return to living in Montreal, hoping to find some freedom and a sense of belonging.

However, what I would find would be worse than everything I had experienced so far. The circumstances leading up to this point provided fleeting relief, but the subsequent events would overshadow the temporary sense of victory. It would mark the end of a promising education and signal the onset of a tumultuous phase that would transform my remaining teenage years into an ordeal.

CHAPTER EIGHTEEN

My New Foster Home

When I requested to be placed in a new foster home in Montreal, my social worker understood that my main reason was to be able to see my brother more frequently. As it was closer, I could go for one night or just visiting during the day and come back. With the subway, it would not take more than an hour to get there. She did agree that I could spend time with him, but only when he was not working. Eventually, she found a new foster home for me close to downtown Montreal. Transitioning to a new environment proved to be a decision I came to regret. The stability and quality of education I had experienced while living with the Martins were nowhere to be found in my new surroundings. Instead of the nurturing environment I had come to expect, I found myself immersed in a setting where drugs were prevalent, and my education suffered as a result. The move derailed the promising path I had been on, leaving me to navigate a world where learning took a backseat.

Sylvie Larivière-Traub

The Legrands, for the most part, treated me kindly, but the rules were strict. After the initial introductions and my social worker's departure, Mrs. Legrand directly explained what I could and couldn't do. I was only allowed to eat during designated mealtimes and forbidden from accessing the refrigerator in between. She made it clear that the financial support she received for my care was insufficient to provide additional food. Another rule was that I could bathe only once a week and wash myself in a sink during the week. Sometimes, if someone was using the only bathroom available, I had to wash myself in the kitchen in front of everyone. Finally, the last rule and probably the hardest for a teenager: I had to come back right from school and could not visit friends after school or early evening, except under strict restrictions. The oldest daughter was in the bathroom for almost two hours almost every night. She had that privilege since she was working and paying her mom weekly rent for room and board. It was difficult for me because Mrs. Legrand's daughters did not have the same rules. However, I had my own bedroom and a television. Lise was a little jealous that she had to share her room with her older sister.

Mrs. Legrand had two daughters, Lise and Monette, and two older sons. However, only the girls remained at home. Lise was around the same age as me, while Monette was about twenty years old. In the first few months, Lise tried to be a friend and include me when going out with her friends, the only time I was allowed to go out in the evening. However, I was only allowed to go out a few times a week, and I had to come back no later than 8 o'clock. Lise, on the other hand, could come back at 10 o'clock. Pretty soon, I realized that I didn't have the same privileges. Mrs. Legrand made it clear that she was responsible for me and couldn't allow anything to happen to me.

During this time, I had permission to visit my brother on some weekends when he was available or not working. I enjoyed going to his apartment and using the shower. Sometimes he picked me up, and other times I took the subway to his apartment. A few times,

I told Mrs. Legrand that I was going to visit Richard. In fact, in those instances, he was not really available. I quickly learned to lie and visit friends instead. My lies worked every time, and Mrs. Legrand eventually trusted that I was genuinely visiting Richard. I believe people were generally more trusting in those days. Also, no cell phone and voicemail made it more difficult to reach people on the phone.

The first summer I was there, Mrs. Legrand took advantage of me for free labor. While she was generally nice to me, she expected me to work during the summer baseball season. The Expos team stadium was one block from us. Since the Legrands had a large area of parking spaces on a corner street, when the Expos were in town, I spent my summer nights holding a poster that read, "Parking space for $2.00." After three to four hours of displaying the poster, I would return with some earnings, but I barely received anything beyond one or two dollars. Although she claimed that she would pay me at the end of the summer, she always reminded me of the burden I supposedly caused them. Of course, I never received anything at the end of the summer, but I knew in my heart that she did not have the money. I swiftly deduced that her husband's struggles with alcohol were likely impacting the cash flow.

I never mentioned any of this to my social worker because I did not want to lose the freedom I had on the weekend. I understood that the financial support Mrs. Legrand received for my care was essential, which likely explained why she had taken me in. Despite this, she genuinely liked me and would talk to me at night when her daughters were away. However, I couldn't escape the feeling of being a prisoner in her home. During that summer, I was limited to staying with her most of the night. Throughout the day, I frequented the nearby public pool, finding solace in the bustling presence of life around me.

I was thirteen years old, soon to turn fourteen, in the midsummer of 1968. It was a rebellious time for the backdrop for my own teen romance. Mrs. Legrand decided to rent a room to a young man in her house. He had striking blond hair and captivating blue eyes and was probably around nineteen or twenty years old. There was an undeniable attraction between us. Every time he glanced at me, my heart raced with excitement. Although communication was challenging, we found solace in spending time together on the front balcony during that first summer. It was a pleasant period that brought a glimmer of happiness into my life.

Against the rules, we managed to concoct a plan and sneak out to see a movie on a Sunday afternoon. We chose to watch *The Sound of Music* in French. Unbeknownst to my date, I appeared older with my height, and my maturity far surpassed the girls of the same age. I believe he did not know my age. The preceding years had been tumultuous, robbing me of my childhood with their tragic events.

Unfortunately, the movie turned out to be quite lengthy, and we had to return home before it ended because I was expected back at a certain time. My date was visibly perplexed and not really happy. Not long after that incident, he made the decision to move out. I was devastated, as I had developed strong feelings for him, and he was a good friend. I can only imagine his departure was a result of feeling uncomfortable with our connection and my lack of freedom to pursue a relationship.

During this time, I still managed to visit my brother on weekends. I loved the moments of freedom I had when I spent time with him and his girlfriend. We would go out together to see movies or go to bars to dance. Because I looked older than I was, he could bring me with him to the bars. In those years, there were shows, live bands, and big dance floors. It was a different era, and no one asked for identification papers.

On the weekends when Richard was working night shifts, I hung out with friends. We would go to the Place of Nations, which had been the official entrance of Expo '67 with flags from all countries. After the exhibition ended, it became a meeting place for young people. Many teenagers enjoyed hanging out there. On Saturday nights we would go there to dance, enjoy live bands, and have a lot of fun. Downtown Montreal was also a vibrant hangout place. Artists, jugglers, and musicians flocked there.

We embraced a bohemian lifestyle, went barefoot, smoked hashish, and experimented with LSD. As my signature look, I painted a flower on my right cheek. Additionally, I started cross-stitching shawls and selling them to earn a bit of money. Our wardrobes mainly consisted of Indian shirts, which we could buy downtown where Krishnas were hanging out, singing and playing rhythm instruments and flutes.

The summer in Montreal during that era was characterized by a vibrant ambiance, with hippies lining the streets, artists performing music and painting, and activists advocating for a Quebec Libre (free Quebec) or protesting Vietnam War, all against the backdrop of the Krishnas.

The following September, I began attending ninth grade at George-Vanier High School. The school had a reputation for being in a tough area. Some of the students were raised in poor and tough neighborhoods. The education was more of a drug's nest education. I started to use drugs more regularly with other students while in classes, and I started to miss classes to have time with my new friends. I did not have any science classes but was put in a general program and started to learn typing. I perceived that studying science was reserved for those who could attend university and sensed that my social worker and Mrs. Legrand held little hope for my prospects.

The lack of interesting subjects at that school and my lack of motivation, combined with the influence of the drug experience movement, caused my homework to suffer and my behavior to deteriorate. I would never complete ninth grade.

CHAPTER NINETEEN

A Rainy Day

Mr. Legrand was an alcoholic. Sometimes, I was left alone with him, and a few times he made inappropriate advances, attempting to corner me on the hallway wall. In these instances, I firmly told him to stop and went to my room. Many times, I cried alone in my bed.

Lise, who I thought was a friend, started to tell me cruel things, stating I would never be part of the family and that her mother liked me, but she would never love me like a daughter. She ended the conversation by arrogantly commenting on how it was sad that I could not go out later than 8 o'clock and go with her and her friends.

That night she really made me cry. I concluded she was concerned about my presence and the attention I was receiving from her mother.

That day, alone with Mr. Legrand, I felt awkward to be there with an old man who was often drunk and attempted to touch me.

Now, Lise was being cruel to me. It was just too much. That night, I thought seriously about escaping.

The following evening, Mr. Legrand was drunk again. I found myself alone with him, and it happened again. I firmly told him to stop, then pushed him away and went to my room, hoping he would not follow me. Once again, I cried alone in my bed. I felt an overwhelming sense of loneliness and abandonment from everyone I had believed cared about me. It was just too much. I couldn't stay there for one more minute.

That night, I decided to leave. I packed a few things in a bag and escaped through the window since the house was on the first floor. I thought that would be the last time I would ever see the Legrands. However, life has its own ideas. Later in my life, I lived in an apartment just a few houses away from them. I reconnected with Mrs. Legrand, who was now a widow. Her husband had drunk himself to his grave. She did not seem to miss him at all. She had not led an easy life, and I had a lot of empathy for her when I learned that her oldest son had died in a car accident a few years before because he was drunk. It was déjà-vu, a sad story of how alcohol can destroy lives and families.

With a heart full of trepidation and anticipation, I finally threw open the window, leaped into the unknown, and raced toward my new destiny. The first night of my escape found me seeking refuge at Lafontaine Park. Raindrops fell incessantly, chilling the night air. The restroom doors were firmly shut, but with determination, I managed to slip into the sheltered entrance, where I found fitful rest.

Morning's early light broke through the clouds, bathing everything in a warm, golden hue. "Thank goodness," I whispered to myself as I stretched and rose from my makeshift bed. The sun's tender rays were a welcome change from the previous night's rain. Eager to explore, I stepped out into the park. Its pathways lay deserted, a far cry from the vibrant gathering of young hippies that I had hoped to find. Undeterred, I set my sights on downtown

Ste. Catherine, a place known to be a hub for young artists and free spirits. May was upon us, promising the presence of a youthful crowd from which I could perhaps find a place to sleep.

Embarking on a journey that combined hitchhiking and leisurely walks, I navigated the city streets, engaging in brief exchanges with the occasional passerby. Amidst the urban landscape, a painter caught my attention. His features were striking, and our conversation flowed effortlessly. Seeking to earn a living from the tourist trade, he proposed a novel idea: painting my portrait in a public space to draw attention. As he captured my likeness, he hoped to entice others to queue for their own portraits. It was a showcase of his skills, an artful display of his talent. That portrait held a beauty that was to be tragically marred by the destructive fury of my first husband. That day, however, marked the beginning of a chapter in my life defined by newfound friendships—a community of artists and kindred spirits who understood my flight from an abusive foster home.

As the summer waned, the need for a more permanent haven became undeniable. By some twist of fate, the authorities hadn't found me. As August ended, a yearning to escape the city's clutches led me northward.

Once again, I began hitchhiking my way to my new life. My brother had a longtime friend in Sept-Îles, about 750 miles north of Montreal. I thought he might be able to help me find a job up there, where it would be hard to capture me.

After a few days of crashing at different places, I was hopeful of finding employment as a waitress and disappearing into anonymity. I adopted a new identity as a seventeen-year-old. It was so easy. I went to the Social Security office and filled in a form with my new name, Sylvie Tremblay, and a new date of birth, after which I received my first Social Security number. There were no computers in those days to verify identities.

My adventure hitchhiking to Sept-Îles was not the easiest one. I had to go through the Canadian Tundra and knew there would not be a lot of traffic on the road leading five hundred thirty miles north of Montreal. This town was located where the St. Lawrence River meets the Atlantic Ocean.

After covering around three hundred and fifty miles, hunger gnawed at my stomach. Only twenty-five cents remained in my pocket. Fate intertwined my path with that of a fellow traveler—a seventeen-year-old with the same aspirations of work and freedom. Our meager resources combined to purchase sustenance, a lowly meal shared between strangers who had become companions on this uncertain journey. As daylight gave way to dusk, an old, welcoming house beckoned from the roadside. Benevolence radiated from the inhabitants, who invited us to their table and provided summer chairs as beds. In the family's warm welcome, I found a respite that invigorated my spirit.

Morning's light broke with a hearty, traditional Quebecois breakfast. Grateful and renewed, we pressed on, resuming our quest for Sept-Îles. That day, fortune favored us—a trucker who was headed to our destination stopped and invited us to go with him. The miles rolled away. As the sun began to set, we arrived in Sept-Îles. We both went to the unemployment bureau.

There, my road companion sought work, parting ways with newfound well-wishes. A few days later, we met again, and he asked if I wanted to leave the town for another destination. He knew I was a runaway and was really afraid to go back to Montreal and back to a foster home. I said no. It made me sad because we were good companions in search of a better life. I also had a crush on him. Later in my life, I always wondered what he was really running away from and how my life would have been different if I had followed him.

The tendrils of fate guided me to my brother's friend, a motel manager who offered me temporary refuge. Though his assistance was modest, it was a sanctuary nonetheless. Employment as a waitress materialized, but my gracelessness was my undoing—coffee cups slipped, plates crashed, and my tenure lasted merely two days.

After a few days at the motel, Richard's friend let me know I could not stay much longer. Disheartened but not defeated, I turned to family living in Sept-Îles—a kinship on my mother's side. Their invitation extended warmth and shelter, and I gratefully accepted. A cousin, only a couple of years my senior, was my confidant, and our bond was sealed with shared secrets.

Yet, the weight of my past choices lingered. My cousin revealed to his parents that I loved drugs. My reliance on hash unveiled my city habits to my small-town kin. The shame weighed heavily on my heart. It led me to flee once again back to Montreal.

Returning to Montreal, I tried to find a companion for my next journey to California. It was a different country, and I was afraid to go on my own; my English was quite poor at the time.

The decision to return to Montreal was not without its regrets. My aunt and uncle were wonderful people who played a significant role in my early years. I loved them dearly, and staying with them would have likely made my life easier. At the time, my reasons for leaving seemed important, but looking back as an adult, I realize they were rather trivial. If I had made a different choice, it might have led me down an alternate road, one of education and comfort with family members, unburdened by the scars that life had yet to etch upon my soul.

Yet, I believe that we are the sum of our experiences. These moments, however difficult, have shaped me into who I am today, and I am at peace with the person I've become.

CHAPTER TWENTY

Fourteen Years Old in an Adult Prison

The crisp air of Montreal was tainted by rain on that fateful morning. Just the previous night I had been lost in the bliss of dancing to late-sixties music at a bar. But the euphoria was short-lived. A sudden police raid interrupted the night's reverie, sending everyone, including me, into a panic. The remnants of the LSD I had taken earlier still raced in my veins, amplifying my anxiety.

Exits were closely guarded, and they asked everyone for identification. Some underage girls were immediately ushered into a police vehicle. I was among them, only fourteen and a runaway from my second foster home. The ominous realization hit me hard: the police were looking for me specifically.

Most of the detained teenagers were claimed by their parents. My fate, however, rested with the youth tribunal. With my past of escaping foster homes, the stakes were high. The judgment came swiftly: I was to be placed in a reception center for troubled youths. But there was no space available. Instead, I was temporarily assigned to Tanguay, an adult women's prison that had recently made provisions for minors. The very idea filled me with dread.

"What kind of person would send a fourteen-year-old girl to an adult prison?" I thought.

In Tanguay, I was stripped of my clothes. A prison guard took me to a dressing room, where I was given new clothes and tennis shoes. Then I was escorted to a unit. Fortunately, the department had only teenagers, and despite the terror, a glimmer of familiarity appeared when I spotted a girl from the bar raid.

Another girl was crying on a chair by herself. Nobody talked to her because she could only speak English. I could speak a little English at the time and sat beside her. I learned she was thirteen years old and American. She was visiting Montreal with her dad when he suddenly died of a heart attack. The hospital personnel called a social worker to take care of her, but she was sent to the teenager unit of the prison instead. It was temporary but an awful place to be for a child. She had nobody to talk to, no friendly environment, and no support. The poor girl lost her dad, and her crime was being alone. The prison I was detained in was the only place they had found for her. Fortunately, someone came for her just a few days later.

The unit the youth were assigned had a great room with tables and chairs for meals and card games. There was a television with additional seating around it. The room opened onto a large corridor with cells on both sides. The doors were painted aqua, which gave the whole area a strange look, somewhere between a prison and a mental establishment. I was given a cell, the first one on the left. It was about fifty square feet with a toilet and a sink. The bed was smaller than a regular single bed.

We were locked in the rooms from 9 o'clock until the morning. The lights were turned off at 10 p.m. The door unlocked at 8 in the morning. During the day we would play cards, talk, or watch the television, which was turned off again at 9 o'clock at night. We were given three meals a day and were allowed cigarettes. Upon request to the guardian, we were given a pack of cigarettes. There was no limit, and we could ask at any time for one more pack.

One day, to my surprise, my mother came to visit. It was one of the rare occasions when she was able to walk with the aid of a cane. She was sad to see me there and could not understand what was happening to me. Until today, I still can remember her crying, probably wondering why she left me at such a young age. It would be the last time I would see her for a long time.

My mother only visited me once during my stay. The sight of her in tears, burdened with a history of health issues and the guilt of decisions made out of desperation, remains etched in my mind. I knew she had been coerced into moving to an assisted living facility, believing I'd be taken care of by my brother. But fate had other plans for me.

What I couldn't have known then was that my stint at Tanguay, as grim as it was, would be a luxury compared to the harrowing experiences that awaited me in the government's other institutions.

CHAPTER TWENTY-ONE

In My Cell with Bob Morane

A few weeks later, I found myself escorted to the reception center for teenagers. As I entered, an austere woman guard, clad in uniform, instructed me to follow her to a small room where she presented me with a set of new clothes.

"You are not permitted to wear your own attire here," she asserted sternly. Reluctantly, I complied and changed into the unfamiliar garments she provided. She commanded with an abrupt tone of voice, "Follow me," and led me towards a staircase. With trepidation coursing through me, I trailed behind her, my mind swirling with questions and anxiety. Why were we descending into the basement? What awaited me there?

At the bottom of the stairs stretched a long corridor, lined with four or five small rooms on the right side. Each door was identical, adorned with a small rectangle window at the top, big enough to peek out from inside the room.

"Get in," the woman guard commanded. Reluctantly, I obeyed, stepping into the room. She closed the door firmly behind me. As the click of the lock echoed in the empty space, a wave of despair washed over me. There was a chilling absence of compassion in her demeanor, leaving me feeling utterly alone and vulnerable. With a heavy heart, tears began to stream down my cheeks.

The confines of the room seemed to shrink around me, enveloping me in a suffocating embrace that sent shivers down my spine. The oppressive atmosphere weighed heavily on my shoulders. In the eerie silence of the room, loneliness wrapped around me, leaving me to grapple with a whirlwind of emotions. Fear and anxiety gnawed at my insides. Questions echoed in my mind, each one more desperate than the last: "Why is this happening to me? What did I do to deserve this?"

With trembling hands, I attempted to gather my thoughts and surveyed my surroundings. The room did not offer any comfort. To my right was a small metal bed with a thin mattress against the wall adjacent to a sink and a toilet. The space felt eerily reminiscent of the cell I had occupied in Tanguay prison, but this room was even smaller, which amplified the sense of claustrophobia and confinement.

Unlike my previous experiences, however, there was no respite from isolation. Confined twenty-four hours a day, seven days a week, with no reprieve or escape in sight, I found myself in a profound sense of despair and hopelessness.

At the far end of the room loomed a solitary window. Its glass was opaque and impenetrable. It was a cruel tease, offering only a narrow slit from which to glimpse the outside world and feel the warmth of the sun. Yet, even in its limited capacity, it became my lifeline, my connection to the world beyond those suffocating walls.

The steel bed frame firmly anchored to the floor served as a reminder of my captivity. It was a deliberate measure intended to prevent any attempt at escape or self-harm. Every bolt and bar seemed to mock my desperation and enforce the inescapable reality of my situation.

But, despite the bleakness of my circumstances, a glimmer of hope flickered within me. One morning, as the first light filtered through the window, a singular thought consumed my mind: when night fell, I would seize the opportunity to pry open the window to grasp at the possibility of freedom, no matter how faint.

From that moment on, my thoughts narrowed to a single, burning obsession: escape. Every waking moment was consumed by the relentless churn of strategies and calculations. By day, I scanned the window frame, searching for weaknesses and rehearsing plans in my mind. By night, I lay in the dark, eyes fixed on the ceiling, imagining paths to freedom. But as each plan unraveled in the harsh light of reality, the cold truth settled in—without tools, the window might as well have been a brick wall.

This plan became more than just a desperate bid for freedom; it became the beacon of hope that kept me tethered to sanity amidst the chaos of confinement. In the darkest moments of despair, when the weight of isolation threatened to crush my spirit, I clung to that hope. It was a glimmer of light in the suffocating darkness, a reminder that there was still a possibility of reclaiming my freedom and autonomy.

As I crafted and refined my strategy with every detail meticulously planned and rehearsed in my mind, I found solace in the act of planning itself. It was a form of defiance against the forces that sought to confine me, a declaration that I would not surrender to despair.

My world shrank to the size of the small room that held me captive. Each day unfolded in agonizing monotony, revolving around the events that punctuated the relentless passage of time. For a fourteen-year-old girl thrust into the unforgiving grip of isolation, even the most mundane occurrences took on a profound significance.

The rhythm of my existence was dictated by the arrival of meals. As the footsteps of the guards heralded the approach of sustenance, a surge of anticipation seized me.

Sylvie Larivière-Traub

The quality of the food that sustained me remains a blur in my memory, lost amidst the haze of confinement and deprivation. Yet, its significance transcended mere sustenance; it became the focal point of my existence, the one event around which my days revolved. I savored each morsel with a desperate intensity, as if by relishing the taste I could momentarily transcend the confines of my reality.

In this barren landscape, time seemed to stretch endlessly before me. These moments of nourishment took on a sacred significance.

Deprived of the most basic comfort, my only seat and my only refuge was the bed's unforgiving surface. With no chair to ease the strain, I'd often sit cross-legged on the rough mattress, my body aching from resting in that position most part of the day. Each day was a battle against discomfort, a reminder that even the simplest comforts had been stripped away. But it wasn't just physical discomfort that tormented me. The absence of fresh air became a relentless source of torment. Each breath I took felt tainted, suffused with the stale scent of confinement that permeated the air.

As the days stretched into weeks, and the weeks into months, I felt trapped like an animal in a cage. I was denied even the simple pleasure of stepping outside, condemned to languish in isolation day after day. The sterile whiteness of the walls seemed to close in on me with each passing sunrise. Solitude became my constant companion, a silent witness to the depths of my despair. In that desolate space, there were no friends to offer solace, no support to lean on, no love to provide comfort.

My childhood, once a time of innocence and wonder, had been warped beyond recognition, transformed into a desolate landscape that bore more resemblance to an adult prison than anything like a home.

My crime? My journey into the justice system began with a crime that, in any other context, would have been seen as an act of self-preservation. Fleeing from the unwelcome advances that took place within the walls of my foster home, I sought refuge. Little did

I know that my flight from danger would only lead me deeper into the throes of adversity.

The bitter taste of familial abandonment was a constant reminder of the fractured bonds that had shaped my existence. From the city center bar to Tanguay prison, and now the Hotel-de-Ville Center, I found myself thrust once more into the unforgiving embrace of authority. A juvenile court nestled on St-Denis Street had reduced the weight of my identity to nothing more than a case number etched onto a piece of paper. In the sterile corridors of justice, I became little more than a statistic, a pawn in a game with rules I had yet to fully comprehend.

The isolation I endured felt like a cruel punishment, a harsh consequence of being abandoned not only by my family but also by the very system meant to protect me.

Amidst the bleakness of my days, a small mercy arrived—a few books, handed to me by my guardian in what must have been a rare moment of compassion. Within those worn pages, I found an unexpected sanctuary. The adventures of Bob Morane, brought to life by the talented Belgian writer Henri Vernes, transported me far from my harsh reality. Once I devoured every word, I cautiously asked the guardian who delivered my meals if she had more from the series. To my surprise, she obliged. In the midst of my grim surroundings, these books offered brief escapes from the harshness that defined my world.

Through the eyes of this intrepid hero, I was transported to realms where possibilities were boundless, where danger lurked around every corner, but so, too, did the promise of adventure. As I devoured each page, I found myself escaping the confines of my physical reality, journeying to distant lands and facing formidable foes alongside Bob Morane.

In the quiet solitude of my room, Bob Morane became more than just a character in a book; he became my steadfast companion. His courage and resilience inspired me to believe that even in the darkest of times, there existed the possibility of triumph.

Sylvie Larivière-Traub

Day after day, as I lay in my narrow bed, I would lose myself in the vivid tapestry of Bob Morane's exploits, allowing his adventures to whisk me away from the confines of my reality. In those fleeting moments, I found solace, hope, and the strength to endure, knowing that within the pages of a book, freedom was always within reach. In the silent depths of my isolation, each day was marked by the turning of pages and the unfolding adventures within the pages in the countless books I devoured. Though I couldn't precisely measure the duration of my imprisonment, I read at least forty books. Once in a while, but still rarely, my solitary confinement was punctuated by the arrival of another girl. In those fleeting moments of connection, through the slit of my window, we could whisper conversations. I found solace in the shared camaraderie of our misery. For a brief respite from the suffocating silence, we whispered our dialogues. Yet, it was the realm of fiction that offered the truest escape from my grim reality. Through the adventures of Bob Morane, I transcended the confines of my prison. His heroic exploits became my own, guiding me through the darkness with the promise of salvation and redemption.

CHAPTER TWENTY-TWO

Out of the Hole

After breakfast, I found myself lost in thought about the misery of my confinement. Each day felt like torture, and I often marveled at how I hadn't lost my sanity. Out of the blue, footsteps echoed in the corridor. Usually, footsteps meant a brief reprieve for a shower or a meal, but today they felt different. I heard a key turn in the lock and quickly sat on my bed. A woman entered.

"I am Sister Laurence," she introduced herself, "I'm here to take you upstairs to join a group of girls." Since my arrest in the bar, Sister Laurence was the first person to be kind to me.

The prospect of finally escaping my isolation and hearing human voices was overwhelming. We ascended to the second floor, where she led me to my new room. Though modestly better than my basement cell, it still felt stark. However, a slightly more comfortable mattress and the tiny window in the door were upgrades. She handed me several royal blue cotton dresses with white collars, a vast improvement from my previous attire, gym shorts and t-shirt.

"Change into this dress," she instructed. "I'll return soon to introduce you to the group." She left and didn't lock the door behind her.

Within fifteen minutes, Sister Laurence returned and led me down a short corridor to a room where six or seven girls sat, chatting. One was knitting.

"You're free to talk here," Sister Laurence began, "but you must avoid discussing the outside world."

It was challenging to abide by these rules, but we had little choice. Among the girls, one named Diane caught my attention. With her short, red hair, pregnant belly, and blue eyes that occasionally flashed violet, she stood out. She discreetly gave me the phone number of the place where she knew she would live once she gave birth. She was risking the establishment's rules. One big subject of conservation was the next meal and the next cigarette we were to have.

We had six cigarettes a day. Three came after each meal, and I enjoyed them with a coffee. A habit I kept in my adult life until I quit smoking. The three other cigarettes were, respectively, around 10:15 in the morning, 3 o'clock, and the last one before going to bed. In those days, it was a great relaxing time and a treat for us.

As days turned into weeks, my life transformed. I no longer dreaded endless isolation. Instead, my days consisted of camaraderie, crocheting, and the anticipation of meals and cigarettes.

One day, I approached Sister Laurence with a request for a book. She granted it, leading me to a dormitory with a bookshelf. Among the titles, one stood out: *La pensée peut tout*! It was a translation of Norman Vincent Peale's *The Power of Positive Thinking*. It became my anchor, teaching me to live one day at a time and to see each moment as a gift.

Sister Laurence started to sit by my bed right before locking the door. She was nice to me and started to encourage me. Her trust in me grew.

The Silent Echo of My Childhood

As Christmas approached, she suggested I organize a festive show for the girls. "You are very creative and have a good imagination. Would you be interested in creating a Christmas show?" I was so surprised someone believed I could do something like this.

With a moment of hesitation, I said, "No. I don't know how to do that." I was afraid of failing.

Sister chuckled brightly and said, "Oh my God, I know you can! You can do anything you want to."

I hesitated, but with her encouragement I accepted. It was great fun. There was a famous song, very popular in those days, called "C'est une poupée qui fait non," translated as "A doll that says no," written by Michel Polnareff. Jimmy Page of Led Zeppelin did the guitar recording in 1966. It became a hit worldwide. The Birds covered the song in English and Jimmy Hendrix did a recording of it in 1967. It was not released officially, but many bootlegs were made of the song.

I decided to create a choreography for the song. Sister Laurence bought me the record. I had girls lined up and practice walking like a doll, sort of an early version of the Michael Jackson moonwalk. We did it for all the personnel during Christmas week.

I felt good about myself and all the applause we received. Sister Laurence loved it so much that the same week she decided I would now sleep in the dormitory. I loved the dormitory. I could even read after the lights were turned off. There was enough light coming from the corridor.

After Christmas, I learned there was a school on the top floor. Sister Laurence thought it would be good if I attended every day. I was very excited. My first day was quite a surprise. It was not a real school. The classroom had desks, but everyone was at a different level. I rapidly became an assistant teacher because the level was lower than what I knew. So, from that day I had a new role, helping teach the ones who had little or almost no education. I learned nothing new during this period. However, it gave me a sense of accomplishment. I had a newfound sense of purpose. Sister

Laurence became my pillar. I later visited her as an adult, and during our reunion, she confided how proud she was of my progress.

But just when things seemed to stabilize, they were upended. A few months after Christmas, officials decided to rotate us between establishments. Sister Laurence regretfully informed me that I was going to the Cite-des-Prairies, called at that time Berthelet.

Leaving behind my books, friends, and newfound role as a helper in the classroom, I prepared myself for Berthelet. I realized Sister Laurence was not just sad about my departure but deeply worried about the challenges I was about to face.

CHAPTER TWENTY-THREE

Berthelet

For some inexplicable reason, my fortunate streak came to an end when the authorities decided to shuffle us to different institutions every two to three weeks. I soon found myself dispatched to the Berthelet Center in Riviere des Prairies, Montreal. This institution was akin to a prison for juveniles.

After numerous upheavals and revolts in such centers, they were permanently shut down in the 1970s, deemed inhumane for children and teenagers. In their stead, the authorities established "improved" institutions, where young minds became the test subjects for psychologists eager to try out novel theories for teenage rehabilitation. My days of good fortune had dissipated and were replaced by the grim reality of confinement in a cold, bar-lined cell where isolation was a twenty-four-hour mandate.

I vividly remember, Wednesdays always meant the same thing—a restless night followed by the inevitable knock on the door. I'd gather my few belongings, knowing the routine by heart. The transfer from the Hôtel de Ville Center to Berthelet had become a familiar rhythm, a constant shuffling back and forth. I never stayed long enough in one place to grow comfortable, just long enough to recognize a face or two before being uprooted again. The purpose behind it remained a mystery until much later—this constant motion, this calculated disruption, was meant to keep us from forming any real bonds, from feeling any sense of belonging.

The memory of my first day there is particularly poignant. It was a foggy morning when we got there. We were sent to a room and told to change into uniforms, and then sent to a unit. There were sixteen cells with steel doors and bars. I was very scared and wondered why I was there and why I was treated with so much hostility, but I had learned not to say a word. I was still that shy teenager, and the only mistakes I made were not having parents who were able to be present in my life, not liking the foster homes they sent me to, and needing to escape from abuse. During those escapes, I could at least have my new friends and enjoy my life with the hippies.

Born in the era of the Summer of Love, I was naturally inclined towards counterculture and the peace movement. Drugs were part and parcel of this lifestyle, believed to "open your third eye." I was never a real delinquent. I was merely a teenager, craving freedom, and yet, the Welfare Tribunal for Youth didn't tolerate it.

Before Berthelet and Hotel de Ville, I escaped one foster home and found life on the streets. Back then, Montreal's streets pulsated with the influx of hippies, artists, and musicians. Although money was scarce, camaraderie wasn't. Albums like those of the Beatles became communal experiences.

However, once the Welfare Tribunal intervened, my life took a sharp turn. I was brought to the first unit on the second floor, where they opened the steel, dark-green cell door and gave me a blanket. That was it. For a bed, a two-inch mattress rested atop a green metal structure bolted to the terrazzo floor. Otherwise, there was simply a small metal locker cabinet.

We were supposed to be let out of the cell for one hour a day to do activities, but it was not happening every day. Most of our time out was happening in the three times a day we went to get our food plates and four times a day to go to the bathroom. And you had better make yourself do it during that time because there was no way they would come to open the cell for you if you needed to go later or were sick. I experienced one time being sick, and it was terrible. I had terrible stomach cramps and required some help. Nobody came that night to help me. I cried in pain all night long.

Despite the stifling conditions, a few bright spots existed. The best time was 8 at night when we could watch a movie and have a cigarette. That was our treat time.

There was no place for humanity in this children's prison. It was what I called the "absence of everything." No friends, no names, no family visits, no love, no one to talk to, no exercise, no books. Just a brutal environment.

When watching television, I always put my legs outside the bars and crossed them together. I also crossed my arms outside the bars. Sitting on the terrazzo this particular way was about the most comfortable posture to watch television. I did not remember that we had any chairs inside the cell.

Among the residents of Berthelet, many were like me, confused and misplaced. During one of my stays that year, a few things went bad. One girl had tried to kill herself. She was put in the hole for one month as punishment. Most of the girls there were social misfits. I guess I was, too, and I still think I have always been. Child protection in those days was far from its supposed mandate. It was more like torture.

One girl, Claire, had a passion for horses. She was a beautiful girl with long, blond hair and big, blue eyes. Constantly subjected to the worst of treatments, she was a constant presence in the dreaded "hole."

Another girl, Denise, often cut on her arms with whatever she could find to write on her arms with her blood. Her scars were a testament to her pain. I don't know how she could have access to harmful objects, but she was found a way. I remember her face, dark hair, deep and sad big brown eyes, and aquiline nose. She looked older than all of us. At that time, I thought she was close to eighteen years old. I don't know how her life turned out later.

Some girls there were tough. I feared them and felt I did not fit in with them. One time, there was a big riot, and almost everyone threw everything they had out of their cells. One of the tough girls was named Linda. She had long black hair and blue eyes and was very petite and skinny. I think she hung out with the Hells Angels and the Devil's Disciples. She was bad and had filthy language.

I felt pressured to participate in the riot, but I didn't want to. I threw one blanket and maybe a pillow. But I felt it was stupid and stopped. The girls were mad at me because I was not throwing the mattress and everything else. They started to call me "Chicken." Linda got all the girls to hate me and called me names, which was a great service she rendered me, even if I did not know it at that time. I did not reply to anyone and sat on the ground, covering my ears. Later on, while I was a student at the University of Montreal, I had the opportunity to read *The Stranger* by Albert Camus. The book fascinated me because Camus could put words to how I felt in the prison for youth. One simple quote: "I opened myself to the gentle indifference of the world." Camus reflects with his character Meursault about his isolation and sense of solitude, capturing the essence of his existential loneliness.

The aftermath of the riot was predictably punitive. We were given ham sandwiches or peanut butter for a month, for breakfast, lunch, and dinner. There was no TV, no movies, no cigarettes. The ones who had thrown away their blankets and mattresses had to sleep on the cold terrazzo. I was very glad that I had kept a blanket, mattress, and one of my pillows. At least my condition was not that bad compared to the other girls. Those who had dispensed with their provisions suffered the most. In Berthelet's gloomy confines, the scant pleasures of food, cigarettes, and television became precious commodities. The worst time was at night; the mattress was terrible and the shadow of the bars on the terrazzo was terrifying. I don't remember how I went through this, but what I know is that I was always thinking of my escape, though I never came up with any concrete plan. Moreover, Berthelet prison was a maximum-security establishment. No way out.

CHAPTER TWENTY-FOUR

The Day of My Escape

The riot became my unexpected exit door from the harsh incarceration. It provided no support, no education, no help, and no protection—ironically, the Government Department Youth Tribunal was under the umbrella of Youth Protection. This was not protection. One morning about three weeks later after the riot, they resumed with normal meals, television night, chocolate bars, and six cigarettes a day. A staff member brought me out of my cell to meet the director at her office. I sat there while she recounted her observations of my behavior during the riot. The director had received a report from the staff explaining that they noticed I didn't participate actively, and even when I tossed away some items, it was more due to peer pressure than involvement. In their eyes, this was evidence that I didn't belong in such a challenging and harsh setting. That was when they decided to transfer me to a low-security establishment as a reward for not fully participating in the riot. I thought it was a good sign for my plan to escape. It was called Carrefour Sylvie, oddly sharing my first name.

Sylvie Larivière-Traub

In this new, atypical setting, a group of girls shared rooms. We carried out daily chores and learned the basics of preparing food. The environment felt more like a home than a reeducation center. Despite their efforts to foster a positive atmosphere, I found it challenging to adapt, even in this comparatively nurturing space. I continued to grapple with the unsettling feeling of being a stranger, persistently alienated from my own family.

Despite the attempt to create a sense of camaraderie with the girls, and the routine of daily chores designed to instill a semblance of normalcy to prepare us to live by ourselves when we reached adulthood, I still felt like an animal in a cage. The struggle to adapt persisted, and the emotional distance from my lost family was like an unbridgeable chasm, which grew wider.

It became increasingly evident that my journey toward a sense of belonging and connection would be a long and arduous one, extending beyond the physical confines of any institution.

One day during my stay there, a peculiar discovery added an unexpected twist to my routine. There was a seemingly inconspicuous exit door on the second floor, just across from the closet that housed the vacuum cleaner. It loomed there, a tantalizing thought of an escape route. The simplicity of it sparked an idea in my head.

Feeling a surge of rebellious courage, I decided to test my luck. On a day when I was assigned to vacuum, I seized the opportunity. Nervously, I ascended the stairs to the second floor and stopped in front of the vacuum closet with a moment of hesitation, stealing glances between the closet and the beckoning exit door. With a spontaneous burst of defiance, I opened the door and was greeted by an unexpected sight—no stairs!

My heart raced as I tried to calculate the distance to the ground below. The surface waiting for me was covered in grass, and a fleeting moment of mathematical reckoning told me that my five-foot-nine-inch height might just be sufficient to make the descent. I steeled myself, held onto the edge at full stretch, and took the plunge. To my amazement, it worked. Dressed in a light blue skirt, a white T-shirt, socks, and tennis shoes, I rose from the grass and felt a bit bruised but miraculously unscathed with no broken bones or major injuries.

I bolted to the street and stood with defiance in the middle, ready to flag down any passing car. The center location on the Montreal River coastline added a geographical layer to my escape saga. The facility was situated north of Montreal, flanked by the River des Prairies and the St Lawrence River to the south, all part of the unique island geography of Montreal.

There wasn't much traffic that morning. A car finally appeared. With my arms moving, flagging the vehicle, I yelled at the top of my lungs, "Stop!" The vehicle came to a halt behind me. I opened the door and got in as fast as I could. I was out of breath. I said hi to the driver, who was probably in his late twenties. I asked him if he could give me a lift because I was running away from a bad situation with my family. "Please hurry—drive away from here," I almost yelled at him. My body shook frantically, and I was scared they had already found out I escaped and would catch me. The driver had no reason not to believe me. I probably looked bad. I told him I could not talk about it as I was too disturbed, but I needed to go to see my mom at her nursing home to seek her help.

He crossed the bridge and left me outside of Montreal. I felt better a few miles away from the center, and I hitchhiked my way to my mother's assisted living home within a few hours.

I was hungry with no money. It was an emotional encounter. I had to tell her I had escaped. I did not want to return to the government establishments, and I asked her to help me.

While I was under government guardianship, my mom was kept somewhat in the dark about my situation. As she welcomed me, she couldn't conceal her concern, sensing that something was amiss with her daughter.

Eager to bridge the information gap and unravel the details of the mystery of my escape, my mom couldn't contain her curiosity. With a mix of apprehension and honesty, I hesitated but eventually revealed the raw truth—I had bolted from the last center, determined to evade the clutches of any place resembling it. The gravity of the situation unfolded in my mom's eyes.

At that moment, as her gaze bore into mine, and I saw not just concern but a profound sadness etched on her face. The circumstances were heavy and complex, and between us, there was an unspoken understanding of the uphill battle I would face ahead.

The last time my mom laid eyes on me was within the unforgiving walls of the Tanguay prison. The mere thought of that place sent shivers down my spine, and I knew I couldn't endure its confines for more than a few hours. The looming specter of the police paying an unwelcome visit to my mother's doorstep added an urgency to my situation.

In an act of maternal love, desperation, and her fear that I would return to one of the government establishments, my mom provided me with what she could. She handed me money, a few items of fresh clothing, and a wig with sunglasses, a makeshift disguise to shield me from unwanted attention. I found some pants in her closet, along with a shirt. We were the same size and height. I rapidly changed into the new clothes, added the wig with sunglasses, and put on some lipstick that she gave me. Before I left, I told her not to worry, that I would go and sleep at my friend Jocelyne's home, adding that I would look for a job and later a room to rent. This was the way I embarked on my uncertain journey. She made a promise to reach out to her network of friends in the hope that they could secure a job for me. I promised I would call her every day.

As I stood on the precipice of an impending struggle—homelessness, scant financial resources, unemployment, and the constant threat of police intervention—my mother's gesture became a flicker of hope in the encroaching darkness. The road ahead was undeniably tough and uncertain, but within that vulnerability, a spark of determination ignited in me. I braced myself for another chapter in my tumultuous journey, knowing that resilience and the unyielding support of a mother's love would be my guiding lights through the storm.

CHAPTER TWENTY-FIVE

Odyssey of the Unexpected

Upon my triumphant escape, Jocelyne, my steadfast companion since our schooldays, welcomed me back into the folds of freedom.

Jocelyne and I were the same age, sixteen. Our connection proved unbroken despite the hardships of my time in foster homes and juvenile detention centers. Reuniting with her was a soothing balm for the wounds of the past; she had not forgotten me. She invited me to stay in her room for a few days. However, she told me it was important that her mother did not know about my presence. I had to hide at night when her mother came back from work. She had no clue about my situation. Jocelyne knew if she had known, she would have made sure her daughter would cut ties with me.

While Jocelyne pursued her educational endeavors, I abandoned the lofty ideal of returning to school. After about a week of staying at her house, her mother saw me and made it clear I was not to stay one more night. Again, I found myself adrift in a sea of destitution, jobless, homeless, and reliant on the generosity of other friends or even fleeting friendships.I compared my situation to Jocelyne's, thinking how she was lucky to have a home and be able to go to school. From then on, my place was on the streets of Montreal, abandoned to my destiny. The whole situation made me sad, and I promised myself one day I would go back to school.

It was during this period that my mother, through her connections, offered a lifeline. One of her friends introduced me to the owner of a small renovation company. He offered me a receptionist and assistant position. My salary was the very small sum of $32.50 per week. I was happy to end up with my first job. However, I fell short of affording bus or metro fares and had to go through a daily ritual of hitchhiking my way to work.

I was introduced on a Monday morning by my mother's friend, and I started the same day. I was excited. For the first time, I could earn my living and rent a room somewhere. My homeless chapter was close to an end.

CHAPTER TWENTY-SIX

A Freedom in Chains

Months had slipped by since I broke free from the confines of the last center where I was sent, Carrefour Sylvie. Evading the relentless pursuit of the authorities had become my art, my survival instinct honed to a razor's edge. With each passing day, I dared to believe that freedom was within reach.

With a hesitant hope flickering within me, I felt a surge of courage to reach out to my social worker. She had been looking out for me since my first foster home with the Martins in St-Eustache. She had always been very nice and caring to me. I outlined to her my newfound stability—a job secured and a first apartment on the horizon. I implored her to leave me undisturbed. To my bewilderment, she responded, "I know where you are, and we've decided to let you go."

Her words echoed in my mind, a cryptic message laden with layers of meaning. How had she known? Was it merely a coincidence, or had someone betrayed my trust? The enigma of her knowledge gnawed at me, a riddle I lacked the clarity to unravel.

Sylvie Larivière-Traub

In hindsight, I couldn't shake the suspicion that my mother, with her quiet strength and unwavering love, had played a clandestine role in my liberation. Her shadow loomed large over my fractured past, a reminder of the family I had lost and the scars that refused to fade. It was a sense of liberation, a new freedom, at last, from the shackles of the prison, but not from the shackles of my past.

The memories of confinement and cruelty were insidious, their grasp unyielding. As I ventured forth into an uncertain future, I carried with me the weight of my past, a burden too heavy to cast aside. And yet, beneath the weight of adversity, a flicker of resilience burned bright—a glimmer of hope that refused to be extinguished.

During my first month of employment, fortune smiled upon me—I found my very first studio apartment. I secured this haven, tucked away in a dismal basement, for a mere fifteen dollars per week. Everything within its confines was draped in shades of brown. The walls wore a tired veneer of fake wood paneling, while the appliances, an avocado stove and refrigerator, echoed the same uninspiring palette. I vividly recall the three words that instantly sprang to mind upon my initial glimpse of the basement, adorned with only a solitary small window: "Brown, Brown, and Brown."

Despite its dreary appearance, the basement dwelling became my sanctuary, a refuge far removed from the confines of my past. It was humble, but it was mine, earned through the sweat of my brows and the meager earnings of my labor. Each week as I paid my rent, I felt a sense of pride, knowing that I had carved out a space to call my own.

In the face of its shortcomings, my apartment symbolized more than just four walls and a roof. It embodied resilience and the ability to transform adversity into opportunity, despair into hope.

The echoes of my past whispered in the back of my mind, but I found solace in the rhythm of my own footsteps, each one taking me farther from the dark corridors I once knew. The sky above felt impossibly vast, a canvas where I could finally paint my own story.

The Silent Echo of My Childhood

The air was different—crisper, more alive—each breath filling my lungs with the promise of new beginnings.

The world unfolded before me like an unwritten book, its pages waiting for my pen. No longer shackled by the iron bars of my youth, I walked forward with the quiet confidence of someone who had tasted freedom after years of captivity. The memory of cold, silent rooms where time stood still faded with each passing day, replaced by the warmth of the sun on my face and the sound of life buzzing around me.

From fourteen to sixteen, my life had been whittled down to a series of locked doors and hushed whispers, the loneliness so thick it was almost tangible. Now, every step I took was a declaration—I was free. The constraints of the past no longer bound me. The world was wide, and for the first time, it was mine to explore.

Despite my pride in my newfound independence and freedom, the weight of loneliness lingered like an uninvited guest. Night after night, the solitude of my apartment became a battleground where haunting nightmares waged war against my fragile peace of mind.

The transition from childhood to adulthood brought with it a heightened sense of vulnerability—a realization that the demons of the past were not easily banished. Instead, they lurked in the shadows, waiting to pounce when my defenses were down.

In the dead of night, as sleep eluded me and the echoes of my unconscious ghosts grew louder, I grappled with the harsh reality of my existence. Alone in the darkness, I faced not only the physical solitude of my apartment but also the daunting task of confronting my inner demons.

Yet, as daunting as the night may be, I refused to let it define me. In the crucible of fear, I discovered the true measure of my strength—a strength forged in the fires of adversity and tempered by the relentless pursuit of hope. As nights unfolded in the solitary expanse of my own dwelling, a harsh truth unveiled itself—I was grappling with the haunting aftermath of my tumultuous story. The eerie stillness of my apartment, once a symbol of autonomy, now metamorphosed into a canvas of nocturnal terror. Darkness draped like a curtain over the stage of my unrelenting nightmares, a theater where the phantoms of my past played their malevolent roles.

Night after night, a ritual unfolded—born of necessity and persistent fear that gripped the recesses of my mind. With trembling hands, I would first cautiously open my closet door, then cast a wary glance beneath the bed, a routine check to ensure that the shadows held no lurking threats. The paranoia was unyielding. On many occasions I would awaken drenched in sweat, my heart hammering like the ominous drums. In the darkness, the nightmares often cast me as a fugitive pursued by an unseen yet palpable menace—a nightly horror show from which there was no escape. Many times, I ran from a person who had a knife. These nightmares were the worst and haunted my nights for such a long time. This nocturnal dance with dread heralded the beginning of an enduring period plagued by night terrors. Each night, an unwelcome unraveling of fears and memories refused to remain dormant. During these vulnerable hours, I often felt like the little girl seeking solace in the hallway or on the piano bench of my mother's bedroom. Now, on the cusp of adulthood, I grappled with a new manifestation of terror, compounded by the memories of countless nights spent in Berthelet, where I drifted to sleep beneath the haunting shadow of cell bars cast upon the terrazzo floor. The ghosts of my past, subdued by day, emerged with a vengeance as night fell, ensnaring me in a nocturnal abyss where reality and nightmares intertwined. Their spectral dance in the shadows cast a chilling pall over my solitude.

CHAPTER TWENTY-SEVEN

In Search of a Family

My friend Jocelyne and I loved going dancing on weekends. There was a bar called the Zebra. It had quite an unconventional setting, and this was where fate introduced me to Andre, a musician. He was a talented saxophone player and was the leader of a band who performed every weekend.

My attraction toward him stemmed from his musical prowess and talent. Artists, particularly musicians, were my weak spot. Unconsciously, I found myself yearning to replicate the tender moments shared with my mother at the piano.

Many times, Andre performed with his band out of town. One day, Jocelyne and I embarked on a grand adventure to visit Andre's band out of town. Without access to a car, we hitchhiked to a town whose location eluded us. We found ourselves relying on the kindness of our ride to not only reach our destination but also provide crucial information about this unfamiliar town.

Our journey brought us to Sorel, where fate took us on a detour through a pig farm. Our ride, a farmer with questionable navigational skills, made a pit stop at his swine sanctuary before reaching our destination. He needed a street book to know where to leave us. We never questioned whether the man had bad intentions when he stopped at his farm. It was another time. Violence had not reached the levels of the twenty-first century.

Jocelyne and I bravely decided to get out of the car for a stretch while waiting at the porcine pit stop. As we stepped out of the car, it became abundantly clear that high heels and pig farms have a strained relationship. The mud beneath us resembled a sinister concoction of farm muck and, undoubtedly, the less glamorous side of pig life.

To our horror, we found ourselves sinking into the quagmire faster than a submarine with faulty buoyancy control. As we struggled in our unintentional swine-themed slip 'n slide, the farmer returned. His response? Laughter. Yes, he found our predicament so amusing that he sauntered back to his vehicle, chuckling at our misfortune. It turns out, the impromptu mud spa we brought in his car wasn't enough to deter him.

The journey to Andre's gig felt like an odyssey, taking us through a labyrinth of twists and turns until we finally arrived. Andre was surprised to see us, and every band member could not believe we had hitchhiked our way there just to see them.

I found myself immersed in Andre's world. Jocelyne got acquainted with Normand, the lead guitarist, who would become her first boyfriend. That night, Andre and Normand decided to pay for a room as they thought it was too dangerous to go back to Montreal hitchhiking. Jocelyne had to invent a terrible stomach problem to explain why she could not come back home that night. The following day, one of the band members brought us back to Montreal, and we finally got back after our two-day adventure.

As Andre and I grew closer, I found myself spending more time at his home, where his family and siblings welcomed me with kindness. He and his siblings lived with their parents. His family was loving, and they cared a lot about me. I immersed myself in their warmth, embraced as one of their own. I juggled my time between their haven and my basement apartment. Andre, at times, played the role of financial savior, by bailing me out and covering the rent so many times. A subtle shift occurred, laying the foundation for a dependence that would grow in the months to come.

Andre was a very good saxophone player. He loved jazz and harbored a trait hidden beneath the surface—a penchant for antisocial tendencies that could escalate into violence when faced with certain situations. Little did I grasp, blinded by my inexperience and the frantic search for love. In spite of his tendencies, he had become my best friend and eased my loneliness.

Eventually, Andre and I decided to take the plunge and share an apartment. At the tender age of sixteen going on seventeen, I was stepping into adulthood. Andre was twenty-seven years old.

CHAPTER TWENTY-EIGHT

A Wild Ride

In the funky year of 1971, Andre and I rented a small studio apartment close to downtown Montreal. Coming out of a fractured environment with no role models, I did not know about normal relationships. This bold move was a questionable life choice as a sixteen-year-old, blissfully unaware of the chaos about to unfold, and Andre was the wise adult with mature thinking, or so he liked to think and I liked to believe. Little did I know, our union was about to become a rollercoaster ride of epic proportions.

The first year we lived together, I ditched my nine-to-five job and hit the road with Andre and his band. Touring life was a wild ride, and it was exciting being on the road all the time and seeing new places. Most of his friends and musicians were drug consumers. Andre and I started to become regular users. It was the beginning of our perilous path of addiction. We tried everything new on the market. Andre had even tried heroin one time, which made him extremely sick.

Sylvie Larivière-Traub

The touring life was exciting. New cities, new faces, with an unusual backdrop of a psychedelic social circle that resembled a rock 'n' roll version of Alice in Wonderland. Everyone was a character, and most of them dabbled in the art of substance experimentation. We were all like explorers charting uncharted territories—except these territories came in little baggies. We were both served a backstage pass to the unexpected world of drugs and rock'n'roll. I had traded my prison for new captors, the psychedelic drugs of the sixties and early seventies.

Andre's band had become very successful and accomplished. Andre entered into a contract with Capital Records (Quality Records in Canada). He entered negotiation with the head of Quality Record Canada for a five-year contract, which would provide an advance of $100,000 in incremental payments, given every year to band members to practice and produce five albums. In the early 70s, that was a lot of money. They were also given a house where they could practice.

This exhilarating journey felt like a whirlwind of stardom, where invitations to glamorous parties flowed freely, and the allure of drugs seemed to follow us like a shadow. It was a period of intense excitement, a cinematic montage of highs. However, the backstage reality concealed a starkly different story.

One afternoon, the usual hum of guitars and drums filled the house, the musicians lost in their own world of melodies and rhythms. But then, without warning, the front door burst open. A group of men, faces set like stone, barged in, their rifles catching the light as they swept through the room. The music died instantly, replaced by a tense, suffocating silence. Eyes darted, hearts pounded, and a cold fear gripped everyone present.

The leader of the intruders stepped forward, his gaze cold and calculating, scanning the room with the practiced look of someone who knew danger intimately. The musicians fumbled for explanations, their voices trembling as they tried to justify their presence in the house. One by one, they managed to convince the men that they were just artists, oblivious to the undercurrents that flowed beneath the surface of their surroundings. The men exchanged glances, a silent communication passing between them, before they slowly backed out, leaving the room as suddenly as they had entered.

The instruments sat untouched for a long time after they left, the air heavy with the lingering scent of gunpowder and the taste of fear. That was the last time they would ever play in that house.

Andre, shaken to his core, recognized that the house was more than just a place to create music. It belonged to a man whose associations ran deep and dangerous—a man whose past was now catching up with him. Without a word, Andre walked away, severing ties with the venture. It was too close, too real. He wouldn't risk getting caught up in a world that could end his dreams before they even began.

Shaken by the ordeal, he distanced himself from Capital Records. In return, the company chose to sign with another band who would later rise to stardom in the French part of Canada with a platinum album. The grand finale had arrived, and the stage was set for a new act. This was the closest he would get to knowing success as a musician, songwriter, and composer. I still kept his songs, which I realize today would have probably become classic rock.

The heady cocktail of drugs, rock'n'roll, and shadows of abuse had seeped into our lives. However, as the applause faded and the echoes of the last chord subsided, the harsh reality of the path to recovery emerged. It was a challenging journey that awaited me, a quest to reclaim a semblance of normalcy from the tumultuous aftermath of our rock'n'roll odyssey.

CHAPTER TWENTY-NINE

A Struggle Over Drug Abuse

Using drugs brought my nightmares and terrors to an unprecedented level. Unlike before, paranoia began to consume me during the day, plunging me into moments of intense fear. I frequently found myself seeking refuge under the bed, gripped by terror at the thought of someone discovering and harming me. The night sweats persisted, now plaguing me at any hour, rendering me incapable of normal function.

An unsettling event unfolded one night while Andre was performing at a Montreal bar. I had just stepped out of the shower, wrapped in a towel, when I heard a distinct noise emanating from the patio door, a subtle yet chilling *cling cling* against the glass. As I approached, I noticed that the window curtain wasn't fully closed. My curiosity turned to alarm when I glanced towards the glass door to see a man staring directly at me.

In a reflexive surge of fear and outrage, I let out a piercing scream that seemed to startle the intruder. Swiftly, he bolted away, descending the cold, steel staircase in haste. The echoes of his hurried footsteps resonated through the night, fading into the distance as my heart continued to race with shock. The intrusion was no help for my nocturnal terrors and paranoia.

Our dependence grew to the point where we sourced the drug from dealers, and Andre began using it recreationally, sometimes experiencing hallucinations. Our drug of choice had interesting names like Angel Dust. We also indulged in Mescaline, mandrake pills, and amphetamine. Aware of the risks, including respiratory decline and overdose, we continued until a terrifying incident forced us to confront the reality of our situation. Andre had ingested a full bottle and was in a blackout state, barely surviving the ordeal. Luckily, I could wake him up and get him to sit. His breathing finally got better, but we knew the incident could have turned out much worse.

This near-death experience shook us, prompting a reduction in our use, driven not only by the fear of dying but also by the increasing difficulty of obtaining the drug. Gradually, we tried to break free from our addiction.

Andre had a friend who had successfully undergone treatments for drug abuse with the help of Dr. Hansen. I consulted him and started weekly treatments. I was prescribed Methaqualone, commonly known in the 70s as Mandrake. Despite its highly addictive nature, this medication offered respite from my terrors, which greatly enhanced my daily functioning. However, I quickly fell victim to its addictive nature, needing higher doses to maintain the relief it provided. Without it, my nightly fears would resurge with alarming intensity.

Excessive use of that drug could cause a decline in the respiratory system. Overdoses, which occur commonly due to an increased tolerance for the drug, could lead to blackouts, coma, and death. We were among the lucky ones to survive it.

The treatment with my doctor partially worked; the paranoia disappeared, but the nightmare terrors persisted. I would have to endure them for the next eighteen years, turning my life into a constant struggle marked by sleep deprivation and haunting childhood memories with the long wait sitting in the middle of the night in the hallways. In 1972, we successfully overcame our struggles with drug abuse.

On November 9th of the same year, I turned eighteen, and ten days later, we got married. The age difference made finding a priest willing to marry us challenging, but we did. The first few years of our marriage were happy, but signs of verbal abuse emerged, foreshadowing the violent turn our relationship would take. Now, the nightmare terrors were sometimes interjected by episodes of abuse and violence.

CHAPTER THIRTY

The Peaceful Period

After we tied the knot, Andre's music scene took a hit with the disco era taking over, leading to a noticeable decline in work and tours. Pre-1972, he was rocking it, constantly on the grind and raking in good money.

I found myself back in the workforce, drawing on the experience from my first job to secure a better position. Simultaneously I decided to go back to school. I skipped finishing high school (a move I always regretted) and jumped straight into college. Turns out, I thrived in that environment. I delved into the history program with some classes in anthropology, balancing work during the day and college at night. Surprisingly, the hectic schedule left me so exhausted that my nightmare terrors took a backseat during this period.

After two years of college, I aimed higher and set my sights on a university degree. I decided to specialize in French Literature, and by the time I was twenty-one, I was enrolled.

Sylvie Larivière-Traub

In a plot twist, Andre, with less work on his plate, decided to join me at the university that same year in the music program. It turned out to be a fantastic period in our married life. He hopped on board with a classical quartet, feeling inspired and intellectually stimulated. We were both riding high on the joys of learning.

Life got even better a few months later when I discovered I was pregnant. Joy overflowed for both of us. With a little girl on the way, we navigated our university schedules, crafting a tag-team approach to ensure we were both there for our soon-to-arrive bundle of joy.

When Melanie made her debut with her entrance into the world, we had our university schedules in sync, alternating days so we could both bask in the joy of parenthood while pursuing our academic dreams.

CHAPTER THIRTY-ONE

Domestic Violence and Abuse

My daughter Melanie was born on April 5th, 1977. I was twenty-two years old. The first two years of her life were filled with joy as Andre embraced his new role as a father with enthusiasm. During my hours of studying in the kitchen, my infant daughter sat contentedly in her chair on the kitchen table, looking at me with my pile of books.

I juggled motherhood with my university studies and spent my summers working at the National Film Board of Canada (NFB). Initially, I undertook interesting projects such as repairing library films and writing synopses. However, as Andre and I completed our degrees, his opportunities for work dwindled. Despite his expectations of more opportunities with his classical quartet composed of fellow students and one of his teachers, such opportunities failed to materialize.

It was during this tumultuous period that Andre showed signs of violence. It was subtle at first, but after a while, he started to use his fists.

Sylvie Larivière-Traub

Andre's increased marijuana and hashish usage only fueled his paranoia, leading to a disturbing fusion of violence and verbal abuse. Desperate to recapture the happiness we once shared as students, I joined Andre in starting a small production company, primarily focused on booking tours and concerts. Despite the challenges, I managed to secure bookings at venues such as malls and libraries, offering a glimmer of hope amidst the darkness. Work seemed to temper his dark side, and the incidents were less frequent whenever he had concerts lined up.

The musician copyright organization initially known as BMI, later renamed SDE, included a division called the Performance Trust Fund. The Fund provided grants for musicians to perform at various venues at no cost to the host. While I handled the bookings, Andre received payment from the Trust Fund for any venues I booked. He even assembled a jazz trio alongside his quartet, all funded through this grant. I secured bookings for classical quartets and jazz concerts. Outside the Trust Fund, I booked regular venues, including performances in bars and a slot for one of Andre's bands at the prestigious Montreal Jazz Festival, in collaboration with Canadian Broadcasting Corporation (CBC).

During this time, I sought solace in painting by enrolling in lessons with different artists. Painting became my refuge and allowed me to escape from Andre's violent outbursts and ease my anxiety. I devoted six to eight hours every night to painting, immersing myself in the creative process. Throughout the first five years of my daughter's life, I painted daily. In the summers I ventured outdoors with my easel, capturing landscapes, churches, and the historic streets of Montreal. Painting became a source of joy and stability in our marriage, offering a respite from the challenges we faced.

It was around 1979 when we acquired a Wurlitzer portable piano, which I began playing. Melanie was demonstrating signs of joy at listening to me like I did with my mom. At three years old, she started piano lessons. Initially, she loved it. However, as the years passed, her father monitored her practice sessions daily, scrutinizing every finger movement and incessantly asking her to repeat passages until she cried. It took its toll. The pressure to excel at such a young age extinguished her natural inclination to play piano. Despite her remarkable talent, praised by her teacher, his overbearing involvement in her practice routine extinguished her enthusiasm.

In the years spanning from 1979 to 1990, the level of violence and abuse within our household reached alarming proportions. Melanie became ensnared in this harrowing cycle. We often found ourselves fleeing to battered women's shelters for safety. On numerous occasions, the police were called to intervene when the tumult of his violence became too loud for our neighbors to ignore. Despite my growing understanding of the vicious cycle we were trapped in from our numerous stays in women's shelters, I felt paralyzed to make decisions and get out of this infernal situation. I was unable to take the necessary steps to shield my child from harm.

The specter of nocturnal terrors still haunted me relentlessly, casting a shadow over my every waking moment. The idea of leaving my husband felt inconceivable; the prospect of navigating life alone with my daughter was daunting and terrifying, eclipsing any fear of the dangers posed by staying with a violent partner. I found myself caught in a vortex of madness, unable to think clearly or act decisively. The fear I had at night made me totally afraid to be alone. The relentless onslaught of violence eroded my self-esteem to its lowest ebb, leaving me devoid of confidence and trapped in a state of despair.

I had swapped foster homes for battered women's shelters, which I began visiting with alarming regularity. Each time, I spent a week in the shelter before returning to my husband with a heart filled with forgiveness. I held onto the belief that my love could change him, that it could coax out the better, kinder man buried beneath his violence. But as the days passed, I watched helplessly as my suffering escalated, and my daughter bore the brunt of the turmoil.

Sylvie Larivière-Traub

Among all the regrets that haunt me, none weigh heavier than my failure to leave my husband sooner, to spare my daughter from the depths of pain she endured. It was a profound mistake.

CHAPTER THIRTY-TWO

Days of Terror

It was early summer 1979; Melanie was two years old. By then, I could sense that something was deeply wrong with Andre. His prolonged silences, the emptiness in his eyes—signs of a brewing storm coming that I couldn't ignore. Sensing the danger, I arranged for Melanie to stay with her cousin Annie for the week. I was grateful she would be away, spared from witnessing the escalating darkness that I felt closing in around us.

The walls seemed to close in on me, transforming our home into a confining cell, eerily reminiscent of the one I had known at fourteen years old. Every step I took felt like walking on eggshells, the tension thick in the air. Andre's silence was oppressive, his presence a constant reminder that an eruption was imminent.

He had been yelling at me and striking me more frequently in recent weeks, but this time felt different—ominously so. Spring had brought a new intensity to his violence, each outburst darker and more menacing than the last. On the morning of the tragic event, he woke up in an unsettling silence, his eyes hollow, pupils darker than usual, as if whatever humanity he once had had vanished entirely. I knew that look all too well—it was the prelude to something terrible. Fear gripped me, knowing that when he was like this, anything could happen.

Beating me was his usual method of release, but sometimes he took pleasure in destroying the things I loved. Once, he broke the frame of a cherished pastel portrait of me painted in my youth and ripped it in small pieces; another time, he crushed a beloved piece of jewelry with a hammer. Other times, he enjoyed destroying with a knife my oil paintings on canvases. It was a way for him to satisfy his rage. His cruelty didn't stop there. He would often bring a knife into the room, placing it beside him or on a table, a silent threat that left me paralyzed with fear. I could not move or even try to leave because I know his rage would become uncontrollable and I could die. He liked to pick up the knife, his gaze turning maniacal, daring me to move. The terror in those moments was overwhelming.

Any reason could trigger him, a phone call, a wrong number, a smile to a neighbor or just talking to a neighbor was enough. We were living near the Little Italy neighbor in Monreal on a third floor.

Suddenly, the oppressive silence was shattered by a sharp loud noise—the sound of his hand meeting my flesh. The impact reverberated through the room, and suddenly, the space around me seemed to shrink, the walls pressing in, trapping me in a cocoon of fear and helplessness. The brutality I had feared had finally arrived, and there was no escaping it.

I curled my body trying to make myself smaller, less of a target. I had reached grim acceptance at some point. My whole body was in pain, and the marks on my skin were the symbol of the invisible chains that binded me. The violence was not only a pattern but each incident left a bigger scar, not just on the body, but on my soul. The house had turned into a battleground where fear reigned supreme. Every slam of the door, every raised voice, sent a jolt of terror through me, a reminder of the constant threat that loomed over our existence.

I waited in silence a few hours until he calmed down. I knew the worse had not happened yet. He was in the kitchen, the knife still at the table. I said to him, "I am going to change." He said nothing and I took my courage and went to my bedroom. However instead of walking to the bedroom, I went to the door entrance, frantically opened the door, and ran down the stairs to my neighbor who lived on the second floor. I knew I was safe if I could get out of the apartment. There were kids on the street playing and parents on their balcony. Once on the second floor, I knew he would not come to get me.

My neighbors were a nice couple, and they knew about the domestic violence. I stayed there all day. They wanted to call the police, but I refused. Andre had told me one time that if I thought of alerting the police at any time, he would kill me. Andre knew where I was, and he came knocking at the door of my neighbor the day after. He asked to see me at the door and looked repentant. He apologized so well that I believe him. My neighbors were afraid for me and did not want me to go, but I decided to go back. However, we had a code that if I was in trouble, I would make noise by jumping on the floor.

I followed my seemingly repentant husband up the stairs, his demeanor calm, almost too calm. But the moment we reached the bedroom, his mask slipped. In a sudden, terrifying shift, he grabbed me by the neck and yanked my long hair, throwing me onto the bed with a force that knocked the breath out of me. Before I could react, I heard the door slam shut, followed by the ominous click of a lock—one he had installed while I was away, anticipating my return.

For two days, that room became my prison. The world outside might as well have ceased to exist. I was trapped, unable to go to work at the National Film Board of Canada or even consider escaping. Every few hours, Andre would burst into the room, his face twisted in a mask of cold, controlled fury, a belt gripped tightly in his hand. Without uttering a single word, he would strike, the belt cutting through the air with a sickening whoosh before landing on my back and legs. Each lash sent waves of pain coursing through my body, but it was the paralyzing fear that gripped me most—the fear that if I tried to resist, this time, he might actually kill me.

I quickly lost count of the beatings, though there must have been at least fifteen. Each strike seemed to grow more vicious, each bruise a testament to his escalating violence. The hours blurred together in a haze of agony and terror, and with each passing moment, I grew more convinced that I wouldn't survive. The thought of making noise, of trying to signal for help, flickered in my mind, but the terror of what he might do if I failed kept me frozen, unable to move, unable to think beyond the next blow.

After nearly forty-eight hours, I realized I had no choice—I had to act. The danger was too real, his violence too extreme. I'd checked the window earlier, hoping for an escape, but we were on the third floor, and there wasn't even a rain gutter to cling to. I was trapped.

But then, a desperate plan formed. I went to the closet and pulled out the shoes that had the heaviest heels I could find. The bedroom floor was bare wood, no carpet to muffle the sound. I took a deep breath and started stomping, hard and fast, pounding the floor with all the strength I had left, hoping—praying—that someone would hear the noise.

It felt like an eternity, but after about ten minutes, I heard a loud, authoritative knock on the door. "We are the police, open the door!" Relief washed over me like a wave. They were here—I though I was saved when Andre, in his madness, tried to dismiss them, telling the officers to leave and mind their own business.

The police broke the door and finally got me out of my misery and living nightmare.

I was taken to a shelter for women victims of violence. It was a place of safety, but like so many women before me, I found myself returning to him after a few weeks. It's hard for others to understand why we go back. The power of an abusive man is insidious, creeping into your mind, making you believe that it's your fault, that you deserve the pain, or that you're simply losing your grip on reality. Over time, they isolate you, slowly chipping away at your confidence until you're a shadow of who you once were.

Yet, amidst the darkness, a glimmer of hope emerged in the form of a psychologist who specialized in treating victims of violence. Recognizing the need for healing within myself, I sought help. It would take a few years of introspection and courage-building before I found the strength to break free from my tormentor.

Domestic violence is insidious, often creeping in under the guise of stress or frustration, but its effects are devastating. It breaks down trust, erodes self-worth, and leaves deep, lasting wounds. The realization that I was living in a cycle of abuse was terrifying. It forced me to confront the reality of my situation and to understand that this was not my fault, nor it was something I deserved.

In the end, it wasn't just the bruises that left their marks—it was the loss of safety, the feeling that no place was truly secure. The violence had shattered more than just the physical; it had fractured my sense of self and my place in the world.

CHAPTER THIRTY-THREE

The Courage to Leave

It was in 1991 that I confronted myself with a haunting question about my marriage and the prospect of leaving my husband. Did I see myself in the same situation when I was older? The resounding answer was no. I could not envision spending the rest of my life on a roller coaster with a person who switched between being nice and normal to suddenly turning into a violent and crazy person.

As Andre's behavior grew increasingly erratic, I began to suspect deeper issues at play. His unfounded paranoia, at times bordering on delusion, suggested, I thought, possible underlying schizophrenia. There were moments when he even accused me of poisoning his coffee with arsenic, a chilling manifestation of his spiraling mental state.

One night, while sleeping deeply in the darkness, I jolted awake to a suffocating sensation. He had pressed a pillow over my face, his maniacal laughter echoing in the room sending shivers down my spine. As I teetered on the brink of unconsciousness, his grip loosened, and he delivered a chilling ultimatum: "If you ever try to leave me, I will kill you."

After a few years of therapy, fear still gripped me, but his control over me had waned. With Melanie, I devised a plan to break free. Secretly, I secured a sub-leased apartment close to Melanie's school. We meticulously packed some clothes and personal effects into garbage bags we concealed in her bedroom closet and prepared for our escape, bracing ourselves for the dangerous possible confrontation that lay ahead.

Since my years in therapy, the frequency of my nightmares had decreased significantly. The nights of waking up drenched in cold sweat, seeking refuge under the safety of my blankets, were becoming increasingly rare, with only occasional remnants lingering. Melanie and I felt poised to embark on a new chapter in our lives.

One morning, summoning every ounce of courage, I woke Melanie early and informed her that today was the day we would leave. We went through our morning routine as if preparing for a typical day: Melanie heading for school and me for work. Andre remained asleep, unaware of our impending departure.

Despite our careful preparations, fear gripped us as we quietly gathered our bags, with the daunting potential consequences of Andre suddenly waking up. My body trembled with panic, tears streaming down my face in silent dread. With shaking hands, we crept to the door, opened it silently, and swiftly loaded our bags into my Nissan hatchback.

"Quickly Melanie, get in the car!" I urged. I stepped inside and shut the door without making too much noise. My hands gripped the steering wheel tightly as I started the engine. Still shaking uncontrollably, I drove away, each mile easing the fear that he would pursue us with frightening speed. He still held a power over me that was overwhelming, a culmination of years of terror.

As the summer sunbathed the world in its warmth, I realized that this morning marked the end of my years of abuse and the beginning of a brighter future. It was the summer of 1991, and I had finally escaped to a better life.

CHAPTER THIRTY-FOUR

The Aftermath

The journey to reclaiming my life was arduous, particularly as Melanie entered the tumultuous realm of teenagerhood. She navigated adolescence with a spirit of rebellion intertwined with a deep-seated resentment towards me for failing to protect her from her father's abuse.

In hindsight, I realize I was ill-prepared to confront these complexities. Haunted by the traumas of my own childhood imprisonment and experiences of domestic violence, I inadvertently subjected Melanie to a similar ordeal. She endured the horrors of witnessing domestic violence, emotional abuse, and incessant criticism. Countless nights were marred by the echoes of her father's violence, leaving her paralyzed by fear and unable to find solace in sleep.

Years later, Melanie confided in me, her voice tinged with the weight of memories she could no longer keep hidden. She spoke of the countless nights she spent alone in her room, tears streaming down her face as she trembled in fear, terrified that morning would come and she would find me lifeless. Hearing her words, my heart shattered. The thought of my little girl enduring such fear, feeling so helpless, was almost too much to bear. It was a pain that pierced deeper than any wound I had ever endured.

Melanie's transition from primary school to Sophie Barrat High School marked a significant shift in her academic journey. While her longstanding friends attended Regina Assumpta private school, my financial constraints prevented Melanie from joining them. Looking back, I regret not finding a second job to afford the tuition, as I believe it could have provided her with a better educational environment and kept her connected with her close-knit group of friends.

Unfortunately, Sophie Barrat High School proved to be a detrimental influence on Melanie. As she struggled to adjust, her attendance faltered, and her grades began to decline rapidly. She began to skip classes and associate with a troublesome crowd. Tensions between us escalated. Despite my efforts to maintain control, I struggled to assert authority and instead attempted to befriend her, a strategy that proved ineffective. It became increasingly challenging to manage her rebellion, especially as her academic performance deteriorated rapidly.

Amidst the turbulence of this period, we sought solace in our newfound freedom. A few weeks after leaving Andre, Melanie and I embarked on a road trip vacation to Virginia Beach. It was a memorable experience, filled with laughter and joy, and it hinted at brighter days ahead. As winter approached, we embraced the season by going skiing together. I was determined to provide Melanie with enriching experiences and foster her love for healthy recreation. While these experiences provided some reprieve and enjoyable moments, the negative influence of her school environment persisted and presented an ongoing challenge.

I felt disheartened, pondering the transformation of my once gentle and kind-hearted daughter. Overwhelmed by a sense of defeat, I decided to focus on my own life. I began attending social gatherings and Saturday night dances in hopes of meeting new companions. However, the relationships I formed were often short-lived and lacked the qualities necessary for a suitable life partner.

Regrettably, there came a point where I felt I had completely relinquished my efforts to guide my daughter through her rebellious phase. Lost in uncertainty, I left her to navigate her challenges alone. It's a decision I've since come to regret deeply, as I realize the lasting impact it has had on our relationship.

A few months after Melanie and I left Andre, I discovered that he had abandoned the apartment we once shared, which left me responsible for the unpaid rent due to the lease not yet expiring. Despite the risks, I made the difficult decision to return and inhabit the space once more.

In the fall of 1992, Melanie and I returned home one night from errands. Unbeknownst to us, Andre lurked in the shadows, hidden among the bushes. In a chilling moment, as I stepped out of the car, I felt a powerful force seize the collar of my winter coat, violently propelling me onto the icy sidewalk below. With Melanie's terrified cries ringing in my ears, I found myself helpless as Andre unleashed a barrage of kicks to my ribs and back with ferocious intensity. Desperately, Melanie attempted to pull me to safety, pleading with him to stop the assault.

As the altercation escalated, Melanie's cries for help echoed through the night, a desperate plea for intervention. Fearing the consequences of being caught in the act, Andre abruptly fled the scene, leaving behind a trail of fear and anguish in his wake.

That harrowing night compelled us to flee the apartment, seeking refuge with a trusted friend for the week. However, our respite was short-lived. Just a week later, Andre's violent actions caught up with him, resulting in his arrest and subsequent imprisonment for a week.

The gravity of the situation forced me to make difficult decisions, including temporarily leaving my job at the Licensing Board of Physical Therapists. The need to hide and protect ourselves from

Sylvie Larivière-Traub

further harm took precedence over all else, compelling me to leave behind the stability of my career to ensure our safety.

CHAPTER THIRTY-FIVE

Making Amends to My Daughter

After the episode of Andre's attack in the fall of 1992, we remained hidden for one year with a friend, Mario, who became my boyfriend. I will always be grateful for his support and help during this transition period. He loved me and Melanie very much, but he was fighting his way to death because of a major alcohol problem. He was there at a good time, but it would be temporary. After one year, we moved out to a new apartment and Mario remained a friend only. It was hard for him because he loved me. However, there was no future. He died not long after from a liver transplant surgery.

After one year staying hidden at Mario's apartment, I returned to work. I did not feel welcome at my work as I had been replaced and they needed to create a new role for me. It did not last long, and I realized I was wasting my talent. There was no recognition, and the salary would never be higher. Finally, I resigned and decided to start my own business in communications and public relations. This is when my life turned in a new direction I had never imagined.

Sylvie Larivière-Traub

Throughout the tumultuous chapters of my life, my daughter Melanie bore the brunt of her father's abuse, enduring unimaginable suffering compounded by my own shortcomings as a protector. The wounds inflicted upon her young soul ran deep, and left scars that cut through the fabric of her innocence. The weight of abandonment hung heavy in the air, a silent specter haunting her every step.

As she navigated the treacherous terrain of her formative years, Melanie grappled with a profound sense of betrayal and disillusionment. The very foundation of trust and security upon which a child relies had been shattered, replaced by a gnawing emptiness and a lingering ache for the love and protection she so desperately craved.

In the depths of her anguish, Melanie's cries for solace often fell upon deaf ears, as I struggled to shield her from the storm raging within our home. The guilt of my perceived failure as a mother weighed heavily on my heart.

Yet, through the darkest of nights and the fiercest of storms, Melanie's spirit remained unbroken. Despite the pain etched into the very fibers of her being, she emerged from the crucible of adversity with a strength and resilience that belied her tender years. Though scarred by the wounds of the past, she refused to be defined by them and forged ahead with unwavering determination and an unyielding resolve to reclaim her sense of self-worth and dignity.

As we journeyed through the labyrinth of healing together, our bond grew stronger with each passing day. Through the tender embrace of unconditional love and unwavering support, we found solace in each other's arms, drawing strength from the resilience of the human spirit. And though the scars of our past may never fully fade, they serve as a testament to the indomitable spirit that lies within us all—a reminder that even in the darkest of times, there is always hope for a brighter tomorrow.

Recently, I've taken steps to make amends with my daughter, though I'm acutely aware that the scars from my past actions linger. Despite our tumultuous journey, the bond of love between us remains steadfast. Together, we strive to embrace the promise of our future, united in our resolve to move beyond the regrets of our shared past. The scars linger, a constant reminder of the trials we've endured. Yet, despite the darkness that once engulfed us, I believe we've both made significant strides toward healing, buoyed by the boundless love we share for each other.

It wasn't until many years later, long after we had begun to confront the violence that had plagued our lives, that my daughter confided in me about the silent tears she shed in her bed, bearing witness to the mistreatment I endured and its ripple effects on her own well-being. Our journey towards reconciliation continues to this day as we strive to navigate our relationship as mother and daughter with love and open communication.

Despite the challenges we faced, our bond has grown stronger over time. Melanie remains my little sunshine, a source of warmth and joy. Today, she is happily married and resides in Maryland with Danny, her husband—a man I've come to cherish as a son. Together, we embrace each other's company, finding solace and strength in our shared journey of healing and growth.

CHAPTER THIRTY-SIX

The Day My Book of Life Becomes Tome 2

Despite the trials and tribulations that defined my journey, I remained unwavering in my pursuit of happiness. Adversity only served to strengthen me and propel me forward on a path toward success, undeterred by the scars of hardship and violence that marked my past.

Following my divorce from Andre, I found myself at a crossroads, grappling with the aftermath of a tumultuous chapter in my life. Yet, from the ashes of that broken relationship, a newfound sense of empowerment emerged, which launched me toward a path of self-discovery and reinvention. With a heart heavy with lessons learned and a spirit buoyed by newfound independence, I embarked on a journey into the exhilarating world of entrepreneurship.

The decision to venture into business ownership wasn't merely a financial pursuit; it was a deeply personal quest to reclaim my life and pursue long-held dreams that had lain dormant far too long. In 1994, I took the bold step of opening my first business, a pivotal moment that marked the beginning of a transformative chapter in my journey.

After parting ways with my job, I took the bold step of forming my first corporation, SL Communications, a venture bearing my own initials. It stood as a testament to my resilience and determination, symbolizing a newfound sense of autonomy and self-determination as I reclaimed my maiden name, Lariviere, shedding the weight of a marital identity that no longer served me.

In those early years of entrepreneurship, I found myself liberated from the constraints that had once bound me in my marriage to Andre. I was no longer confined by the expectations and limitations imposed upon me and reveled in the opportunity to explore my skills, talents, and passions with newfound freedom and autonomy. It was a period of profound growth and self-discovery while I navigated the exhilarating highs and daunting challenges of business ownership with fearless determination and resilience.

Over the course of four years, I poured my heart and soul into running my company. Each day brought new opportunities for learning, growth, and innovation. As I honed my entrepreneurial skills and navigated the complexities of the business world, I found fulfillment in the pursuit of my dreams and the realization of my potential. It was a time of flourishing, both personally and professionally, as I embraced the exhilarating journey of building and nurturing a successful enterprise.

Through perseverance and determined resolve, I emerged from those formative years of entrepreneurship stronger, wiser, and more empowered than ever before. And while the journey was far from easy, the lessons learned and the experiences gained during those years laid the foundation for a future filled with endless possibilities and boundless potential.

While financial prosperity may have eluded me, the success of my business afforded me invaluable opportunities, from indulging in trips to the Caribbean to securing my first home, made possible by a modest inheritance from my father's cousin. I was able to provide for my daughter in a much better way. Our annual vacations became a cherished tradition with four consecutive years spent exploring the shores of Virginia Beach. This venture into entrepreneurship marked a significant milestone in my life, a new chapter filled with promise.

As I navigated the complexities of running my own business, Melanie embarked on her own journey into the workforce and carved out a path independent of the traditional routes of college and university. However, amidst the triumphs of my professional endeavors, Melanie grappled with the same demons that had haunted me in my youth. She bore the burden of domestic violence's aftermath, serving as a poignant reminder of the cyclical nature of trauma and the profound impact of intergenerational struggles. Yet, in the face of adversity, she remained steadfast in her belief that redemption was possible.

In time, Melanie found success in her career and returned to school to complete her high school degree, pursue higher education, and ultimately graduate with honors from the University of Toronto with an Honours Bachelor of Science (HBSc). Year after year, our relationship blossomed, filled with mutual pride and admiration for each other's achievements. I am immensely proud of her accomplishments and grateful for the bond that continued to strengthen between us.

My struggles were far from over as I would later embark on a business partnership that would unveil the darker aspects of human nature. It would become a life lesson in how individuals can be swayed by the temptations of wealth and greed and how even the most respected institutions can become tainted by corruption.

In the ensuing years, I would encounter individuals reminiscent of Gordon Gekko, the iconic character portrayed by Michael Douglas in *Wall Street*, with his infamous mantra: "Greed is good." Regrettably, I would come to realize that reality often eclipses fiction. I witnessed firsthand the pervasive influence of unchecked greed and the detrimental impact it can have on individuals and society.

CHAPTER THIRTY-SEVEN

Turning Tides: From Adversity to Triumph

It was a fateful encounter that would forever alter the course of my journey. In the year 1997, I crossed paths with Pierre C., a man whose brilliance was only matched by the tumultuous nature of his personal struggles, particularly his battle with alcoholism. Yet, amidst the chaos of his tortured existence, there burned a fierce and unyielding spark of creativity—an indomitable spirit that refused to be extinguished by the demons that plagued him.

Pierre was more than just a man; he was a visionary, a trailblazer whose restless mind brimmed with ideas that defied convention and pushed the boundaries of possibility. Despite his ongoing alcoholism, he possessed an uncanny ability to channel his creative energies into tangible creations, bringing his visionary concepts to fruition with astonishing clarity and precision.

The product he introduced to me, "Faces: The Ultimate Composite Picture," was nothing short of revolutionary—a groundbreaking advancement poised to redefine the landscape of facial imagery for years to come. With its unparalleled capabilities in facial recognition and composite imaging, it held the promise of transforming the way law enforcement agencies approached the fight against crime.

From the moment I laid eyes on Pierre's creation, I knew that I had stumbled upon something truly remarkable—a product that transcended mere commercial value and spoke to a deeper sense of purpose and passion. As someone deeply committed to the cause of crime prevention and justice, I recognized the immense potential of Faces to make a meaningful impact in the world.

Driven by a shared passion and vision, Pierre and I embarked on a new venture together, fueled by a commitment to harness the power of technology for the greater good. Our focus was clear: to cater to the unique needs of law enforcement agencies by providing them with cutting-edge tools and solutions to combat crime more effectively than ever before.

Despite the challenges that lay ahead, our partnership thrived on a shared sense of purpose and a relentless dedication to excellence. Together, we forged ahead, navigating the complexities of the business world with determination and resilience, fueled by the knowledge that our work had the potential to make a lasting difference in the fight for justice.

In Faces, I found not only a groundbreaking product, but also a symbol of hope for crime victims, guiding us forward on a path of innovation.

Despite the brilliance of his concept, the realization of Pierre's vision hinged on securing substantial investments to propel the product towards completion and eventual market launch. Recognizing the pivotal role I could play in bringing Pierre's dream to fruition, I made the bold decision to invest two thousand dollars of my own capital into the venture, securing a significant stake in the company's private stock.

However, my involvement went far beyond mere financial backing. Eager to lend my expertise and support to the endeavor, I also assumed the role of a consultant for the company, leveraging my skills and experience to provide strategic guidance and direction. It was a multifaceted commitment that required balancing my responsibilities between my own business and my newfound role within Pierre's company.

Though I had never previously raised capital or written a formal business plan, I approached the challenge with enthusiasm. Recognizing the importance of securing additional funding to fuel the project's development, I embarked on a journey of self-education and skill development, immersing myself in the intricacies of fundraising and business planning.

Through countless investor presentations and meticulous updates to the company's business plans, I honed my abilities in the field, cultivating expertise that would prove invaluable in navigating the complexities of the startup landscape. Each pitch, each iteration of the business plan, served as an opportunity for growth and refinement, allowing me to expand my knowledge base and sharpen my entrepreneurial acumen.

Despite the steep learning curve and the inevitable challenges that arose along the way, I remained undeterred in my pursuit of excellence. With a steadfast commitment to the success of the venture, I embraced my newfound role as a catalyst for progress and innovation, channeling my passion and drive into every aspect of my work. As I continued to evolve and grow, I found fulfillment in the knowledge that my contributions were helping to bring a transformative vision to life—a vision that had the power to revolutionize an entire industry and make a lasting impact on the world.

CHAPTER THIRTY-EIGHT

Meeting the America's Most Wanted Team

In 1998, a pivotal moment emerged in the trajectory of our enterprise as we caught the eye of a significant stakeholder—a well-known Quebec venture capitalist—drawn in by the promise and potential of our groundbreaking technology. As we sought to amplify our reach and secure influential endorsements, one name loomed large in our aspirations: John Walsh, the revered TV host of *America's Most Wanted* on Fox.

We had already secured the endorsement of Child Find Canada and the accolades of the Royal Canadian Mounted Police (RCMP). Armed with confidence and determination, Linda T., the President of Child Find Canada, and I embarked on a mission to secure an appointment with him or his publicist, recognizing the transformative impact his endorsement could have on our venture.

Despite our persistent efforts to reach out via phone calls, our attempts went unanswered, met with nothing but silence. Undeterred by setbacks, I made the decision to take matters into my own hands, orchestrating a bold move that would bring us face to face with our desired contact.

Together with Linda, I journeyed to Bethesda, Maryland, mere miles from Washington, D.C., close to the office of John Walsh's publicist, Avery Mann. We approached the office building intent on making our presence known and our mission clear. However, upon arrival, we were met with an unexpected obstacle—a stern-faced guard stationed at the entrance, his role seemingly to deter unwanted visitors.

Our determination refused to be quashed. With a renewed sense of purpose, I turned to Linda and declared, "Let's head to the hotel and keep calling until someone answers." In that moment, we were fueled by a shared resolve to leave no stone unturned in our quest to secure the endorsement we so fervently sought.

Linda, resourceful as ever, had managed to uncover the elusive information we needed. She had a contact with the National Center for Missing & Exploited Children—an organization formed in the wake of John Walsh's unimaginable tragedy, the abduction and murder of his six-year-old son, Adam. Avery Mann, John Walsh's publicist, was no stranger to Linda or the cause she championed.

With a background in criminology and a passion for justice, Avery Mann embodied the very essence of the mission we were striving to advance. Linda knew him through John Walsh's National Center for Missing & Exploited Children. They had been in contact through their respective organizations. It was a stroke of fortune that she had been in contact with Avery through Child Find Canada, providing us with a crucial contact in our pursuit of securing an audience with John Walsh himself. Armed with Avery's contact number, we wasted no time in making our intentions known. With each repeated dial of the phone, our anticipation grew, fueled by the knowledge that we were on the cusp of a potentially life-changing opportunity.

Finally, after many attempts and as the phone rang on the other end, there was Avery Mann's voice, warm and welcoming, greeting

The Silent Echo of My Childhood

us on the other end of the line. In that instant, our perseverance was rewarded. My thirty-second elevator pitch with Avery Mann worked. "Can you come to the office this morning?" he asked. Not even within a second, I replied, "We can be there in seven minutes." That day, we set the wheels in motion for what would become a pivotal meeting, one that would later cement our partnership with John Walsh and pave the way for the realization of our shared vision to make a difference in the world.

As Linda and I stood outside the studio of *America's Most Wanted*, anticipation crackled in the air, mingled with nervousness. The mere thought of stepping into the halls of one of television's most iconic shows left us both awestruck.

Upon entering the studio, we were greeted by the sight of a modest office space, a far cry from the glitz and glamour we had imagined. Yet, in that unassuming setting, we found ourselves on the threshold of an encounter that would change the course of InterQuest forever.

Avery, John Walsh's esteemed publicist, welcomed us with warmth and grace, introducing us to another production team member. With trembling hands, I opened my laptop, the weight of expectation heavy upon me as I prepared to unveil our software product to these esteemed industry professionals.

As the demo unfolded on the screen before them, showcasing the mesmerizing process of morphing one celebrity's face into another, a hush fell over the room, broken only by the soft hum of the laptop's fan. Avery and Michael watched in rapt attention, their expressions a mixture of astonishment and delight.

"Hold on," Michael exclaimed, his excitement palpable. "Let's gather everyone in the conference room. This is something they need to see." We followed Michael into the conference room, interrupting the production meeting. After a brief introduction, I launched the software demo once more, in front of a room that buzzed with anticipation. The members of the production team were leaning forward in their seats, captivated by the transformative power of our technology.

As the demo drew to a close, they welcomed our product with excitement and enthusiasm. In that moment, we knew that we had struck gold—that our technology had the potential to revolutionize the industry and capture the hearts and minds of audiences around the world.

And so began a partnership that would defy expectations and transcend boundaries. *America's Most Wanted* embraced our product wholeheartedly, recognizing its value as a powerful tool in the fight against crime. It was the beginning of a strong business relationship—one that would propel us to new heights of success and visibility in the years to come.

CHAPTER THIRTY-NINE

In the Spotlight

During subsequent visits, we articulated our ambitious vision to establish a worldwide standard for future products in facial recognition technology. Despite being a small company based in Montreal, Quebec, we were unwavering in our commitment to making a global impact. Our strategy was audacious yet simple: to invest in giving away a single license copy of our software to fifty thousand police precincts across Canada and the United States.

As our business relationship with *America's Most Wanted* blossomed, we set plans in motion for the production team to visit our office in Quebec. The goal was to shoot a segment for the show highlighting our generous donation and showcasing our technology. This segment would also underscore our dedication to supporting law enforcement agencies in their crucial work.

The concise segment, close to ten minutes in length, would also feature the creation of a composite picture of a wanted criminal in Florida, who had been terrorizing communities in Florida with acts of child molestation. It was a somber reminder of the stakes involved in our mission, and the profound impact our technology could have in bringing perpetrators to justice and safeguarding vulnerable populations.

As the cameras rolled, the composite picture took shape before our eyes. And then, in a stroke of serendipity, our efforts yielded immediate results. The first composite picture we created struck a chord with viewers, resonating deeply with a grieving mother, who recognized her own son as the perpetrator. She called the America's Most Wanted hotline to let the staff know about her son. It was quite an amazing event.

In the aftermath of the show, the phone lines buzzed with tips and leads as viewers across the nation rallied to support the cause. The success of our first-time use was nothing short of a triumph; it was a home run.

With hearts full and spirits buoyed by our early success, we were welcomed into the *America's Most Wanted* team, united in our shared mission to make the world a safer place.

During this pivotal juncture in our company's journey, we found ourselves in pursuit of another substantial investment—an infusion of at least one million dollars to propel our product's marketing efforts in the United States. Faced with this daunting task, we turned our attention to Quebec Union Funds, with whom we began negotiations.

Fortunately, our endeavors received a significant boost from the National Research Council of Canada, which generously provided grants to support our research and development endeavors. Their endorsement of our technology bolstered our credibility in the eyes of potential investors.

It was against this backdrop that the Quebec Funds expressed interest in our venture, intrigued by the promise and potential of our innovative product. However, despite their initial enthusiasm, they remained cautious, unfamiliar with our company and its founders. However, they were very impressed by our success on the south border and the free coverage we had on a major American television show, a first in Quebec.

In an effort to mitigate their apprehension and secure their investment, we struck a deal: If we could secure the official endorsement of John Walsh and *America's Most Wanted*, the Funds would commit to investing one million dollars in exchange for a twenty percent stake in our company.

At the time, this deal seemed like a golden opportunity—an injection of much-needed capital in exchange for a relatively modest ownership stake. However, in our eagerness to secure funding, we failed to fully comprehend the implications of such an arrangement and the potential pitfalls that lay ahead.

Unbeknownst to us, the Funds had their own agenda, driven by motives that were not entirely aligned with our own. Their willingness to invest hinged precariously on the attainment of John Walsh's endorsement, a condition that would later prove to be a double-edged sword.

As we eagerly forged ahead, buoyed by the prospect of securing the necessary funding to propel our company to new heights, little did we know that we were about to embark on a journey fraught with challenges and unforeseen obstacles. And as the true nature of the deal with the Funds began to unravel, we found ourselves grappling with the harsh realities of the business world.

With anticipation, Pierre and I embarked on a pivotal journey to meet with Lance Heflin, the executive producer of *America's Most Wanted*, and his trusted long-time partner John Walsh. Our mission was clear: secure their official endorsement for our product, Faces. As we presented our case and outlined the transformative potential of our technology, Lance Heflin and John Walsh listened intently, their expressions a mixture of curiosity and intrigue. John Walsh rarely endorsed any products as he was firstly an advocate for the victims of crime. He felt his mission could be a conflict of interest.

To our elation, though, they agreed to throw their support behind Faces, granting us the coveted endorsement we had sought.

Sylvie Larivière-Traub

At that moment, a wave of euphoria washed over us, our excitement barely contained as we hastened to share the momentous news with the Funds representative, Robert, and the rest of our team. It was a triumphant testament to the power of collaboration and conviction in the pursuit of a shared vision. I don't think the Funds expected our success.

After our donation to police precincts, the marketing of Faces marked the beginning of an extraordinary journey—a journey that would catapult us into the spotlight and thrust our innovative product into the global spotlight. John Walsh became the spokesperson of Faces, captivating audiences with his impassioned advocacy for our technology. Across the nation, press conferences were held in every city where the show was shot as John Walsh eloquently championed the transformative potential of Faces in the fight against crime.

In Canada, our triumph truly took center stage as we found ourselves thrust into the spotlight through newspaper headlines and media frenzy. We were hailed as the creators of one of the most groundbreaking technologies in Canada, and our innovative product captured the public's imagination and garnered widespread acclaim. Prestigious prizes and awards soon followed, further solidifying our status as pioneers in the field of facial reconstruction and imaging.

Amidst the whirlwind of attention and accolades, we remained steadfast in our commitment to advancing the cause of justice. With Faces at the forefront of our mission, InterQuest forged ahead with unwavering determination, fueled by the knowledge that our technology had the power to change lives and make the world a safer place. As we basked in the glow of our success, we knew that the journey was far from over—indeed, it was only beginning.

The media attention extended far beyond the confines of traditional print. Invitations poured in from across the airwaves, beckoning us to share our story on the hallowed stages of French television. From the esteemed *Claire Lamarche* show to other prominent programs, our product became a familiar sight to viewers across the nation.

The Silent Echo of My Childhood

As our appearances on television captivated audiences, the momentum of our success surged beyond the borders of Canada. Soon, the spotlight of international acclaim beckoned. From the iconic stages of the *Leeza* show in Hollywood to the revered studios of *The Maury Show* at NBC in New York City, our journey from humble beginnings to global recognition unfolded before us. Our presence on these esteemed platforms served as a testament to the profound impact of our technology on a global scale.

Yet, amidst the glitz and glamour of the spotlight, we remained steadfast in our commitment to advance the cause of justice and progress. Our journey was not merely one of personal triumph, but of collective achievement with the support of our partners and collaborators. And, as we stood on the precipice of a new era of innovation and possibility, we knew that the best was yet to come.

Amidst the whirlwind of media attention and accolades, another significant opportunity emerged on the global stage. During the same period, I had the privilege of meeting with representatives from the World Customs Organization in Brussels, Belgium, who expressed keen interest in having me present our groundbreaking product to all member countries the following year. It was a momentous occasion, a presentation to more than one hundred countries, as our technology was poised to revolutionize not just local law enforcement but international security efforts as well.

However, while our vision gained traction internationally, challenges brewed closer to home. The Funds, accustomed to managing traditional manufacturing companies, struggled to grasp the nuances of our innovative marketing strategy tailored for the software industry. Our emphasis on establishing standards worldwide and preparing to sell licenses for each patrol car in North America and Western Europe seemed foreign to them, so they didn't understand our pricing approach.

Amidst this backdrop of progress and potential, a threat emerged from within. The Funds representative, Robert, a narrow-minded and morally compromised employee, whom we referred to as "Sharpy," conspired with a few misguided allies within our own company to orchestrate a hostile takeover. It was a betrayal that blindsided us, threatening to derail the very foundation we had worked tirelessly to build.

Despite our suspicions, we kept moving forward. We were determined to overcome the obstacles in our path and continue our mission to revolutionize the industry.

As the challenges mounted and the shadows of betrayal loomed larger, doubts began to creep in, casting a pall of uncertainty over our once-promising venture. The weight of the Funds' million-dollar investment in a Quebec company felt like a burden, a deal signed in blood that now seemed more like a pact with the devil himself.

The opponent we faced seemed to embody all the malevolence and cunning of a force beyond human comprehension. Their corruption ran deep, weaving its tendrils into every facet of the business landscape we navigated. It was a revelation that shook us to the core, challenging our understanding of the lengths to which greed and deceit could extend.

With each passing day, we found ourselves teetering on the verge of regret, questioning the wisdom of our decisions and the integrity of those we once trusted. The prospect of facing off against such formidable adversaries seemed daunting, and we struggled to fathom the depths of their depravity and the extent of their reach.

Yet, even in the face of such adversity, a flicker of determination remained. We refused to succumb to despair, rallying our resolve to confront the forces against us. Though the road ahead appeared treacherous, we clung to our naive belief that "good" would prevail and that our perseverance would ultimately lead us to triumph over the darkness that threatened to engulf us.

CHAPTER FORTY

A Trip to Japan

In 1999, amidst the swirling currents of a turbulent period, with sights set on market expansion and securing vital investments, I embarked on a few months' journey to Tokyo, Japan. It was a pivotal moment, a convergence of fate and opportunity that would forever alter the trajectory of our enterprise.

In Tokyo, I had the privilege of being introduced by my friend Alan Pratt, president of Crime Stoppers International, to Mr. Toshiaki Ogasawara, the owner of *The Japan Times*. Alan arranged for a meeting followed by lunch at his penthouse atop the newspaper building. As we ascended to his apartment, I was struck by the breathtaking panorama that greeted us.

The penthouse exuded an aura of refinement and sophistication. Every corner showed off Mr. Ogasawara's impeccable taste and appreciation for art and history. Antique vases, their delicate beauty preserved through the ages, stood sentinel alongside exquisite paintings that captured the essence of bygone eras. Sculptures, masterpieces of craftsmanship, whispered tales of empires long faded into memory, their silent presence lending an air of reverence to the space.

Mr. Ogasawara welcomed us with warmth and grace. Over the course of our conversation, we delved deep into the intricacies of his beloved country and its intricate relationship with the United States, a bond forged through mutual admiration and shared values.

A man of extraordinary intellect and ambition, Mr. Ogasawara's educational pedigree spoke volumes. He studied at the prestigious University of London before furthering his academic pursuits at Princeton University. His vast array of interests and accomplishments and his entrepreneurial spirit extended beyond the realm of journalism, encompassing ownership of Nifco, a prominent manufacturer of plastic automotive fasteners.

The Japan Times, under Mr. Ogasawara's stewardship, stood as a beacon of English-language journalism in Japan, offering a vital conduit for cultural exchange and dialogue on the global stage. As we discussed the potential for collaboration and partnership, I was struck by the depth of his insights and the magnitude of his vision, which resonated deeply with our own aspirations for growth and impact.

A self-made titan with humble beginnings, Mr. Ogasawara's rise to prominence was nothing short of remarkable. He had forged an empire in the bustling metropolis of Tokyo, his endeavors spanning industries and continents. My own encounter with Mr. Ogasawara's world was nothing short of surreal—an unforgettable experience. Alan arranged for a lunch at the Japan Times building's opulent penthouse, where I found myself in the company of Mr. Ogasawar's closest team, dining amidst an atmosphere of elegance and refinement. It was a moment of profound awe and gratitude—a glimpse into a world far removed from my own, yet strangely familiar in its warmth and hospitality.

Following a sumptuous business lunch that tickled the senses with an array of culinary delights, Mr. Ogasawara graciously arranged for a journalist to interview me. As the afternoon sunbathed the penthouse in a warm, golden glow, I found myself immersed in conversation, sharing the story of our journey with Faces and the vision that propelled us forward. It was a moment of connection and camaraderie as we delved deep into the intricacies of our innovative technology.

The following morning, as I looked at *The Japan Times* over a steaming cup of green tea, I was greeted by a sight that took my breath away. There, emblazoned across the cover in bold letters, was a familiar face and my name—the culmination of an extraordinary journey that had brought me halfway across the world. It was a moment etched in my memory. The accompanying article, penned with eloquence and insight, praised the ingenuity of our technology and the promise it held for shaping the future of innovation. It was a validation of our tireless efforts and a testament to the belief that Mr. Ogasawara had placed in our company's potential.

During my trip to Tokyo, amidst the bustling streets and towering skyscrapers, Mr. Ogasawara reaffirmed his commitment to our cause with a gesture of unparalleled generosity: He decided to invest $500,000 U.S. dollars in InterQuest.

As I reflected on the events of my trip, I was filled with a profound sense of gratitude and humility. In Mr. Ogasawara, I had found not just an investor but a partner. As I prepared to bid farewell to Tokyo and the memories we had created, I carried with me a renewed sense of purpose and a deep-seated belief in the power of collaboration.

As I journeyed back to Montreal, buoyed by the exhilaration of my recent exploits in Japan and coming back with a major investment firmly grasped in my hand, I couldn't help but feel a surge of excitement coursing through my veins. The prospect of returning home to brag about our triumphs on the international stage filled me with pride.

With eager anticipation, I wasted no time in relaying the exciting news to my partner Pierre, eager to share the fruits of our labor and the promising prospects that lay ahead. The money, swiftly transferred to our company's broker, served as tangible evidence of the success of our endeavors and the burgeoning potential of our technology.

Tragically, the significance of Mr. Ogasawara's monumental investment was eclipsed by the machinations of those whose vision for the company diverged from our own. Despite his generous support, Mr. Ogasawara found himself facing forces that sought a different trajectory for our enterprise—a turn of events that would alter the course of our journey irreversibly. He trusted me, and he did not want to invest in the company without me and Pierre. I kept it secret from the Funds, the Chairman, and major investors, knowing they would do anything to gain Mr. Ogasawara's trust. I knew the product would go nowhere without the visionary that was Pierre.

CHAPTER FORTY-ONE

A Hostile Return from Japan

The company we had meticulously built from the ground up, inching ever closer to the success we had dreamed of, was suddenly and violently wrenched from our grasp. Those we had once trusted revealed their true colors—insatiable greed masked by false camaraderie. What followed wasn't just a hostile takeover; it was a ruthless act of betrayal, stripping us not only of our shares but of the very essence of our livelihoods.

It all began with our partnership with Whalen Beliveau to secure major investments and take the company public on the Canadian Stock Exchange. For months, we poured our hearts into preparing for the launch, envisioning the bright future that lay ahead. But during a crucial Board meeting, the representative from the Quebec Funds delivered a blow we hadn't anticipated. They coldly announced that the Funds had reached a consensus: they would exercise their veto power to block the company from going public. This veto right, buried in the fine print of the agreement we had signed when they invested a million dollars, became our death sentence. It quickly became clear that their true intent was far more sinister—they wanted to oust us, replacing our team with their own puppets.

We would later learn that this was their modus operandi: eliminate the visionary founders, install their own management, and seize control. But they underestimated Pierre. Without his direction, the company's future was doomed, no matter who was at the helm. Investment bankers, brokers, and investors alike were stunned, watching in disbelief as a group of opportunistic thugs took control, oblivious to the vision that had brought the company to the brink of greatness.

In the midst of this turmoil, I was plunged into a darkness I had never known. The dream we had nurtured, the company we had cultivated with such passion, lay shattered at our feet—a casualty of corporate treachery. Yet, even as despair threatened to consume us, a spark of defiance flickered within. We were determined to reclaim what was rightfully ours, to rise from the ashes of this betrayal stronger and more resilient than ever before. For in the fires of adversity, true strength is forged, and our determination blazed even brighter in the face of overwhelming odds.

As the takeover's aftermath unfolded, loyal employees who had been with us since the beginning faced the grim reality of unemployment. The company, once poised to go public, was now adrift, its future uncertain and its direction lost.

But the betrayal went deeper. Using fraudulent means and underhanded tactics, they sought to bury the positive developments I had brought back from Japan, to obscure the bright future that was within our grasp. They fabricated false documents, accusing Pierre of crimes he had never committed—claiming he had been imprisoned. It was a lie, a desperate move to remove him from power, and I, his closest ally, was swept away with him.

The agreement we had with the Quebec Funds, the one that brought in a million dollars, had given them a veto right. It also allowed them to strip shares from anyone involved in criminal

The Silent Echo of My Childhood

activity. They didn't need to strip our shares, though. Instead, they used this fabricated accusation to terminate Pierre and me, casting us out of the company we had given everything to build.

As the full magnitude of their betrayal became clear, I grappled with a storm of emotions—anger, disbelief, a profound sense of loss. Yet, amid the chaos, one thing remained unwavering: our resolve to weather this storm. United in our determination, we vowed to overcome this adversity and safeguard the future of InterQuest, no matter the cost.

CHAPTER FORTY-TWO

A Rebirth from the Ashes

Under the new management of InterQuest, all endorsements went away: John Walsh, Child Find Canada, Mr. Ogasawara in Japan, and all potential licensing deals. The company spiraled into decline. I had to make a very difficult decision: withdraw Mr. Ogasawara's investment and ask Whalen Beliveau to promptly return the funds, along with the accrued interest. Mr. Ogasawara's disappointment was palpable, and he struggled to comprehend the motives of the Quebec business investors who had tarnished their promising collaboration. He had championed our business in Japan, forging connections with the Tokyo Police Department, who welcomed our technology with open arms. He was extremely disappointed in the Funds, and I do not think he was ever to do business with Quebec again. It was pathetic. The news of the hostile takeover reverberated across the United States like a shockwave, prompting our law enforcement allies to hastily distance themselves from the new management. Even the prestigious FBI at Quantico, where I had once delivered a lecture to an audience of forty international visiting chiefs of police, now turned their backs on the company in the absence of its founders.

In the tumultuous aftermath, Pierre and I waged an arduous battle to reclaim control of our technology before it was irreparably tarnished and cast into oblivion. With determination burning in our hearts and a steadfast resolve to preserve the integrity of our vision, we fought tooth and nail against the forces of corruption and betrayal, refusing to relinquish our dream to those who sought to destroy it. For months we fought them. One year later, a major lawyer's cabinet found their subterfuge and told them the criminal record they had was false. They knew it was false, but they never thought that one of the largest Montreal law firms would confront them.

In a bold move to confront the Funds, we issued a stern ultimatum to its president, threatening to expose their deceitful practices to the unforgiving glare of the press, thus unraveling a scandal of unprecedented magnitude. I vividly recall the relentless pursuit of the Funds' president as I obtained his personal cellular phone number and dialed it repeatedly, disrupting his rounds of golf. Despite his steadfast refusal to engage with me directly, the pressure I exerted to unearth the truth behind the Funds' Machiavellian machinations and their orchestrated hostile takeover proved to be an unbearable weight. Faced with the imminent threat of the scandal erupting into the public, they recoiled in fear.

In a feeble attempt to mitigate the fallout from their egregious actions, they brazenly proposed returning the technology they had callously destroyed, albeit for a paltry sum of one dollar. Their audacious offer came with the condition of signing a binding non-disclosure agreement, designed to cloak their deceit in a shroud of secrecy. This gesture, veiled in the guise of reconciliation, only served to cast a stark shadow of fraudulence over their actions, exposing the depths of their duplicity. Pierre and I signed a non-disclosure agreement, one of the conditions to get back our technology, and we moved to the United States to restart the company, in California, where we received help from the California State University and its Criminology Department that helped us restart from the ground. I never considered this agreement legal. They gave us back the technology because of their wrongdoing, and they knew I could go public with the story at any time.

This chapter unfolded against the backdrop of my already fraught relationship with the Quebec government during my youth, with yet another major institution in Quebec betraying the trust the people bestowed upon it. The echoes of past disappointments reverberated with a haunting familiarity as I grappled with the bitter realization that the very institutions meant to safeguard our interests had become agents of betrayal and deceit.

Once we reclaimed our technology, disheartened investors rallied to inject fresh funds into our venture, spurred by a profound sense of indignation at the lies and deceit propagated by a major stakeholder, the Funds. With their support, we embarked on the arduous task of rebuilding from the ashes of betrayal.

The company bore the scars of significant damage, its once-bright prospects obscured by the cloud of deception. Police departments, erroneously assuming our demise, had turned their gaze elsewhere, necessitating a painstaking journey to regain their trust and re-establish our credibility. Yet, fueled by a relentless determination to prove our resilience, we embarked on this uphill battle.

Undeterred by the obstacles before us, we pressed on, reaching out to police departments across the United States to herald our revival. Through our tenacity and perseverance, our software gradually began to reassert itself, reclaiming its rightful place at the forefront of crime-fighting innovation.

In the adversity, we changed the name of InterQuest to IQ Biometrics. A lot of law enforcement organizations knew about the scandal and would have never done any business with InterQuest. Once we changed the name, I called all the organizations to let them know we had regained the technology. John Walsh was excited by the news. Throughout this tumultuous period, stalwarts of our cause such as John Walsh of *America's Most Wanted* and Lance Heflin, the executive producer, remained steadfast in their support, standing shoulder to shoulder with us in our darkest hour. Their commitment was more than symbolic; they actively lent their expertise and influence, cementing their place on our new board and helping to chart the course for our potential rebirth.

Despite the weight of our losses, both financial and emotional, our determination remained resolute. With renewed vigor and a steely resolve, we set about laying the groundwork for our revitalized enterprise. Establishing a modest foothold on the south shores of Montreal, we opened the doors to our new office, imbued with a sense of hope and purpose. It was here, amidst the tranquil hum of daily operations, that we sowed the seeds of our very challenging resurgence.

CHAPTER FORTY-THREE

9/11

These events transpired prior to September 11th, a date that would etch itself into history with tragic significance. I had scheduled meetings with investment bankers at the World Trade Center; yet I found myself grappling with mixed emotions regarding the impending trip. Despite my initial resolve, overwhelmed by recent events and countless sleepless nights, I made a fateful decision.

The exhaustion that weighed heavily upon me, both physically and mentally, left me drained and in desperate need of respite. Consequently, I postponed my journey and promptly canceled the appointments with the investment bankers that had been meticulously planned for September 11th.

Little did I know that by altering the course of my plans, I had unwittingly averted a cataclysmic fate. On that fateful day, the very day I was originally slated to be present at the World Trade Center, tragedy of unimaginable proportions would strike, forever altering the landscape of our world.

Sylvie Larivière-Traub

We had an exhibit scheduled to commence on September 16th—a showcase of Faces that held immense significance for our company's resurgence. The chosen venue for this momentous occasion was also none other than the iconic World Trade Center. In the days leading up to September 11th, our team worked tirelessly to ensure that everything was in place for the exhibit. On the Friday prior to the tragic events that would unfold, our company diligently shipped the necessary equipment and a towering giant screen to the New York Port Authority.

These preparations symbolized more than just logistical arrangements; they represented our collective determination to rise from the ashes of adversity and seize the opportunities that lay before us. Curiously, on September 11th, all our showcase equipment mixed into the rubble of the World Trade Center.

CHAPTER FORTY-FOUR

The Aftermath of 9/11

The tragic terrorist attack on September 11th ushered in a new era of policies and politics. We now found ourselves battling not only criminals but also terrorists. The Fresno State University Department of Criminology played a crucial role in facilitating the swift transfer of our business to Fresno, California, due to the urgency sparked by the events of September 11th. Our technology had the potential to combat terrorism.

Amid this struggle, the Fresno Department of Criminology and the president of Fresno State University extended their aid. Recognizing our vision and the potential impact of our products in the fight against crime, they urged us to relocate to Fresno, California. Timothy S. of the Fresno Business School generously provided us with space in their Business Incubator, joining a chorus of voices appalled by the injustices we had endured.

Hence, we made the decision to move our office to Fresno, California, propelled by the immense support from the Fresno State University Department of Criminology. My mission was to establish operations and open the American office. Holding a one-year visa in the United States, I secretly hoped to extend my stay. This was the time we started negotiating with Lockheed Martin in Alabama and with the Microsoft Public Safety Department for a groundbreaking collaboration—an innovation that had the potential to revolutionize the fight against crime and terrorism.

Tim Stearns extended a helping hand to facilitate our transition and provide us with the necessary infrastructure to rebuild. It was through Tim's connections that we were introduced to Eric M., an alumnus of Fresno University whose office was situated in the bustling hub of Cupertino. With a formidable background in venture capital, Eric wasted no time in extending an offer to guide us through the complex process of going public on Nasdaq and securing key investors.

One such pivotal investor, Greg M., emerged on the scene with a staggering one million dollars, mirroring the remarkable support we had received in Quebec. Yet, as history seemed to repeat itself, we soon found ourselves navigating familiar terrain, fraught with challenges and uncertainties. While a portion of the investment was earmarked for research and development, it wasn't long before we realized that we had relinquished control over both the funding and the management team.

One Friday morning, I asked my secretary to get me all the financial statements on my desks for review. On Monday morning, I arrived at the office with a sense of anticipation, only to be greeted by a chilling sight: all the locks had been changed, effectively barring me from entry. It was a scene reminiscent of our past struggles, except this time, the adversaries we faced were emboldened by the influence of the Silicon Valley elite.

Before long, it became apparent that they had orchestrated yet another maneuver to oust us from the company. However, this time, I had fortified myself with a signed contract featuring a parachute clause—a provision designed to safeguard my interests in the event of separation from the company. Despite the reassurance of this legal safeguard, my hopes were dashed as they callously disregarded the terms of the agreement.

Furthermore, they stripped all the original shareholders in Montreal of their rightful stakes in the company. While half of the original shareholders who had placed their faith in our vision remained on paper, the essence of their involvement was hollowed out, their voices drowned amidst a sea of new faces. The once-familiar roster of shareholders vanished, replaced by a cadre of Eric M.'s associates and business partners, leaving us disheartened and disillusioned again.

Their approach was orchestrated on a grand scale, marked by a cunning scheme designed to lure unsuspecting entrepreneurs with the promise of going public. Employing a tactic that seemed all too familiar, they insidiously insinuated that our company was small, obscure, and in need of a merger with a purportedly more robust entity. Under the guise of enhancing our value, they persuaded us, much like countless other entrepreneurs, to forfeit a significant portion of our shares in exchange for the illusion of greater worth.

However, the grim reality soon revealed itself: the company we were coerced into merging with existed only in name, a phantom entity fabricated on paper with artificially inflated numbers. As the magnitude of their deception dawned upon me, I couldn't help but draw parallels again to the nefarious exploits of Gordon Gekko in *Wall Street*. Yet, in the face of such brazen deception and manipulation orchestrated by these high-level con artists, even Gekko's notorious reputation paled in comparison.

This time, despite the tumultuous events, I managed to hold onto my stock. However, the victory was bittersweet, overshadowed by the protracted legal battles that ensued. For over two years, I found myself locked in a relentless struggle with lawyers on both sides of the border, fighting tooth and nail to reclaim what was rightfully mine. Yet, as the dust settled and the legal fees piled up, the harsh reality set in; the value of my stock had plummeted from a promising $2.5 million to a mere $1.2 million.

After settling my attorney bills in both Canada and the United States and paying my taxes, less than half of the initial amount remained. A devastating blow, not just for me, but for all the Canadian shareholders and American consultants who found themselves deprived of their rightful shares in the company. It was a sobering reminder of the ruthlessness of corporate warfare and the toll on those caught in its crossfire.

It was around this time when I met my future husband, Daniel Traub. It felt like a beacon of light amidst the darkness. In him, I found solace and companionship, believing that I had finally transcended my past and childhood challenges.

From the moment our paths crossed, I knew I had found my soulmate, and every moment I spent in his presence was imbued with joy and contentment. Daniel was not just a husband; he was my rock, my confidant, and my greatest source of strength. As a father and stepfather, he embraced his role, showering our family with boundless love and affection.

However, as life would have it, the profound losses of loved ones, including my beloved husband, would awaken the dormant wounds of abandonment buried deep within me. Despite the years of happiness we shared, the pain of separation would reignite these deeply entrenched issues, casting a shadow over my heart and soul once more. Yet, even in the midst of sorrow, I remain grateful for the love and memories we shared, forever cherishing the profound impact Daniel had on my life and Melanie's.

CHAPTER FORTY-FIVE

The Day I Left My Beloved California – Part 1

"Keep love in your heart. A life without it is like a sunless garden when the flowers are dead." —Oscar Wilde

It's July 7th, 2021, and the weight of twenty long months since Daniel's passing presses upon me. Before my eyes, a twenty-seven-foot trailer looms, stationed conspicuously in front of my home. Only yesterday, two hired hands lent their strength as we carefully loaded all my possessions. Amidst the flurry of activity, I strive to redirect my focus towards the dawn of a new chapter in my life.

Over the past two years, a profound realization has settled within me: I am no longer shackled by the fear of solitude. The cavernous void and suffocating sense of abandonment, once omnipresent, have gradually waned. Each step forward marks a triumph over my grief.

Yet, as I stand on the precipice of change, uncertainty shrouds my future like a thick fog. Doubt gnaws at the edges of my resolve as I question the wisdom of my decision to relocate to Florida. Weeks of meticulous packing have distilled memories into tangible artifacts: personal mementos, cherished photographs, and the accumulated remnants of eighteen years shared with Dan. Today, as I bid farewell to this place, emotion weighs heavily upon my heart. I know that amidst the sun-drenched streets of California, fragments of my past will linger, a bittersweet reminder of the life I leave behind.

Nestled along the sun-kissed shores of Hollywood Beach stands the cherished beach cottage, a timeless sanctuary steeped in the rich tapestry of Daniel's family history. It is more than just a house; it is a repository of memories, a vessel carrying the echoes of laughter and the whispers of generations past.

Enveloped by the salty sea breeze, the cottage had been a steadfast fixture in Daniel's life, a beacon of joy and solace. While not directly perched upon the sandy expanse, its proximity to the shore—merely 150 feet away—imbued it with an intimate connection to the cerulean horizon beyond. We affectionately dubbed it the "Happy Place."

The legacy of the cottage stretched back to the early sixties when it first graced the family estate. Throughout the summers, it served as a haven for Daniel's grandparents, a place where time seemed to stand still amidst the gentle lull of the waves. For Daniel, it was a repository of cherished memories, a treasure trove of childhood adventures and carefree days spent exploring the sandy shores.

Each time twilight descended, the rhythmic cadence of the waves became a symphony of serenity, serenading us with its soothing melody. It was a nocturnal lullaby, a reminder of the enduring bond between man and nature and the timeless beauty of the sea. After his mother's passing in 2016, Daniel inherited the cottage and became the steward of its legacy and the guardian of its stories, ensuring that its hallowed halls would echo with laughter and love for generations to come.

The ocean beckoned to us early in our marriage, casting its spell upon our hearts with an irresistible charm. My lifelong dream of owning a sailboat came to fruition when Daniel, committed to my happiness, unearthed a gem—a modest twenty-eight-foot sailboat that would become our vessel of dreams.

Our maiden voyage, however, showed our novice seafaring skills. Our eagerness eclipsed our experience, leading to a comical

The Silent Echo of My Childhood

mishap as we careened towards the dock with all the finesse of first-time sailors, not being able to slow down the boat. The resounding thud echoed our inexperience, leaving us red-faced and sheepish amidst the laughter of onlookers.

Yet, adversity merely steeled our resolve. When news arrived of our beleaguered boat sinking into the depths, we were quite sad. However, with determination born of love and a shared dream, we rallied. Summoning a tow and mustering every ounce of optimism, we embarked upon a journey of restoration.

For two months, our sailboat languished in the care of skilled hands at the repair shop, undergoing a metamorphosis from dilapidated wreckage to seaworthy vessel. With each passing day, our anticipation grew, fueled by the promise of new adventures on the horizon.

Finally, the day arrived when our beloved boat emerged from its cocoon of repairs and, restored to its former glory, beckoned us to the open sea again.

Recognizing the importance of safety and preparedness, we devoted ourselves wholeheartedly to mastering the intricacies of sailing. We underwent comprehensive training, which equipped us with the knowledge and skills necessary to navigate the unpredictable waters of the ocean. From mastering the art of stopping the boat at sea for rescue operations to honing our ability to navigate by the light of the stars, which we really never mastered, we left no stone unturned in our quest for proficiency.

Our efforts bore fruit swiftly as we embarked on a day sailing trip close to the Channel Islands, where the azure waters beckoned with promises of adventure and discovery. We finally got to a point where we navigated the rolling waves with the ease and grace of seasoned sailors. But amidst the challenges and triumphs, it was the laughter and camaraderie shared aboard our humble sailboat that truly enriched our experiences. Through its modest accommodation, our sailboat emerged as a steadfast companion, effortlessly sailing the Hollywood Beach areas.

Sylvie Larivière-Traub

The Channel Islands had always been notorious for their unforgiving weather conditions. From unpredictable currents and shifting swells to sudden bouts of fog and fierce winds, the elements in the channel were known to change with alarming rapidity, which presented a formidable challenge to even the most seasoned sailors. Our sailboat, though sturdy and reliable, was deemed ill-equipped for such treacherous waters, particularly when confronted with the daunting task of traversing California's bustling shipping lanes. The Channel Islands had that reputation that the wind could turn on a whim.

Venturing into these waters demanded a level of skill and experience that we, as relatively inexperienced sailors, knew we lacked. However, we had good training at the Club, and Dan was capable of maneuvering in troubled waters. Yet, one fateful day as we found ourselves battling against the elements with Melanie by our side, the full extent of the channel's fury was unleashed upon us.

The wind howled and the swells surged, catching us off guard as our sailboat teetered precariously at a sharp angle, the sail strained against the force of the gusts. In a heartbeat, disaster struck as the wind tore through the fabric of our sail, leaving us vulnerable and adrift amidst the tumultuous sea.

But in our moment of panic, Daniel remained calm. Drawing upon the training we had received from the esteemed Channel Islands Sailing Club, he remained steadfast and composed, his actions guided by a steady hand and a clear mind. With deft precision, he swiftly lowered the jib and main sails, alleviating the strain on our vessel, before igniting the four-stroke motor to propel us toward safety.

As the chaos subsided and the shore loomed ever closer, a profound sense of gratitude washed over us, tempered only by the awe-inspiring bravery and skill displayed by Daniel in the face of adversity. In that moment, he transcended the role of mere sailor and emerged as our protector and hero.

CHAPTER FORTY-SIX

The Day I Left My Beloved California – Part 2

The journey through grief was a harrowing one, fraught with pain and sorrow that seemed to stretch into infinity. Before Daniel's passing, our hearts had already weathered a series of devastating losses, each one leaving us reeling. It began with the somber vigil of Daniel's mother. Her presence was a beacon of strength even as she faded away in the embrace of hospice care within the walls of our home. Six months later, we were once again plunged into mourning with the passing of his stepfather, Robert, a loss that felt like the severing of the last remaining tether to a bygone era. And just when we thought we had weathered the worst of the storm, fate dealt us another cruel blow with the sudden departure of my beloved big brother, Richard, in April 2018.

Around 1972, Richard's presence faded from the everyday rhythm of my life. He got married and moved away, the distance creating a quiet void where his laughter and companionship had once been. I visited him once in approximately ten years. But then, one day in the early eighties, he returned. I helped them search for an apartment, and I was so happy to see him again. It was as if time had folded in on itself, and we slipped back into our old ways, the bond between us rekindling effortlessly. We never talked about that terrible day that two men came to get me. I was mad at him for a long time but found a way to forgive him. I regret not having talked about the reason why he did that before he passed away. I never had a clear picture and would have liked to know for closure.

With each loss the darkness seemed to deepen, enveloping us in a suffocating embrace that threatened to consume us whole. Yet, even in the depths of our despair, there was a flicker of resilience, a stubborn determination to persevere. And so, with heavy hearts and tear-stained eyes, we forged ahead, clinging to each other as we navigated the treacherous waters of grief.

Each loss carved a deep jagged wound in our hearts, leaving us raw and vulnerable in its wake. The aftermath was a tumultuous storm of grief and confusion as we struggled to come to terms with the sudden absence of those we held dear. Their memories lingered like ghosts, haunting the corners of our minds and echoing in the hollow chambers of our hearts.

In the somber silence that followed, we were left to grapple with the tangible remnants of their lives, each object a poignant reminder of our losses. Sorting through their possessions felt like a mountain looming before me.

Boxes upon boxes filled with cherished mementos and bittersweet memories crowded our living space. Each item was carried with a story, a fragment of a life now gone, serving as both a comfort and a cruel reminder of what I had lost.

Each passing day dedicated to sorting through the remnants of their lives, I found myself unable to stem the tide of tears that welled up with each cherished object I packed away. But amidst the overwhelming grief, I began to find moments of light and hope that served as beacons guiding me towards healing and acceptance.

Though the pain of their absence would always linger, I took comfort in the knowledge that their memories would forever live on in my heart. As I faced the daunting task of moving forward, I clung to the memories of those I had lost, drawing strength from their legacy, and forged a path toward a brighter tomorrow.

I had poured my heart and soul into transforming the Traub family beach cottage into a haven uniquely my own, infused with a delightful blend of beachy vibes.

I now prepared to leave it, standing at the threshold of a new chapter in my life.

My beloved Havanese dog, Einstein, will accompany me on this bittersweet journey. With meticulous care, I equip my trusty Buick Encore for the road ahead, ensuring Einstein's comfort with his cozy car bed and favorite toys, alongside essential travel bowls for water and food. The car itself bears the weight of precious cargo, filled with treasured memories, carefully nestled in the rear.

Amidst the haze of grief, my husband found himself the heir to a precious legacy—the beloved beach cottage. Purchased by Anna and Frank Owens, Dan's grandparents on his mother's side, in 1962, the cottage held a storied history of the laughter and warmth of countless summer vacations.

For a modest sum of $6,000, Anna and Frank secured not just a house, but a sanctuary—a "Happy Place" where the cares of the world melted away beneath the golden rays of the sun. It was here that children frolicked in the sand, built castles and memories that would endure a lifetime. I recall my husband fondly reminiscing about the idyllic summers of his youth, his dreams of one day retiring to this cherished haven echoing in our conversations. Tragically, fate intervened, cutting short his life prematurely, leaving behind lingering sorrow and the painful realization that we will never have the opportunity to grow old together as we had once hoped.

Sylvie Larivière-Traub

With each passing year, the cottage stood as a silent witness to the ebb and flow of life's ever-changing tides. And though the road ahead remained uncertain, the promise of returning to the "Happy Place" lingered, guiding us towards a future filled with the warmth of cherished memories and the promise of new beginnings. Dan thoughtfully hired a contractor to build a charming art studio with a quaint Dutch door adorned with window box flowers. It served as a sanctuary where my creativity could flourish. We did live at the beach cottage from September 2018 till his passing, and I remained there until July 2021.

Yet, in my grief for my passed loved ones and the enduring absence of my beloved husband, the allure of Oxnard Shores, with its rugged coastline and pristine beaches, lost its hold on me. The prolonged lockdown imposed by the COVID-19 pandemic cast a pall over the state, which drove many businesses to shut down and leave the once vibrant community.

Amidst the echoes of bygone laughter and whispered promises of dreams deferred, I found myself at a crossroads. Though the decision to depart from this place of solace was tinged with sadness, it also imbued me with the hope of new beginnings and the promise of finding solace in a world forever changed by loss and longing.

Parting ways with a significant chapter of my life feels like bidding farewell to the very essence of my being—eighteen cherished years woven with the threads of love, laughter, and the unwavering presence of an extraordinary husband. "Oh God, how I ache for you, my dearest," I whisper into the void, consumed by the haunting absence of my beloved. "Why did you leave me stranded in this sea of memories, utterly adrift and alone?"

Today the familiar walls of our beach cottage serve as a cruel reminder of the chains that bind me to the past—a relentless prison of memories with no escape in sight. Once again, I want to break free from the shackles of grief and forge a new path forward.

Relocating away from California is not borne solely from the desire to flee the ghosts of my past but also from the pull of family

The Silent Echo of My Childhood

ties—my daughter's presence on the East Coast calling me to new horizons and fresh beginnings. Yet, amidst the anticipation of a new chapter unfolding, a heavy burden weighs upon my heart—the knowledge that my beloved Dan rests peacefully beneath the shade of a magnificent tree near our beach cottage.

The thought of leaving his side fills me with overwhelming guilt, as if by departing, I am betraying the sacred bond we shared. The prospect of fewer visits to his final resting place casts a shadow over my resolve, leaving me grappling with the conflicting emotions of longing for Dan and guilt, torn between honoring his memory and embracing the promise of a future yet unwritten.

With a heavy heart, I step through each room one last time. The walls echo with the laughter of Christmas gatherings past, the gentle strumming of my husband's guitar, and the sound of his voice filling the air with songs.

I finally muster the courage to close the door on this chapter of my life, each click of the lock sealing away a trove of cherished memories. It feels as though I am locking away a piece of my heart.

With a bittersweet smile, I acknowledge the "for sale" sign standing sentinel in front of the house. Though this physical space may soon belong to another, the memories it holds will forever reside within me. I carry them like precious gems, treasures to be revisited in moments of quiet reflection.

With tears glistening in my eyes, I gently settle my faithful companion, Einstein, into his bed beside me, finding solace in his presence.

As I prepare to depart, I cast one last wistful glance at the house that has been my sanctuary but also witnessed my husband's last breath.

I am leaving for a long journey that spans the breadth of the country. I set out from California to Florida with a brief stopover at my daughter's eagerly awaited new home.

As I navigate the winding roads that stretch before me, I find comfort in the familiar strains of Tom Petty's melodies, a nostalgic reminder of the countless adventures I shared with Dan. Together, we had reveled in the joy of the open road, our voices mingling in harmony as we sang along to our favorite tunes.

As the miles pass away beneath my wheels, the weight of his absence grows heavier. The music that once brought us such joy now serves as a painful reminder of all that has been lost. I try to focus on my new home in Groveland, Florida—a place where memories of the past will mingle with the promise of a brighter tomorrow.

My journey starts with a frustrating trudge through the congested streets of Los Angeles and the maze of traffic surrounding the San Bernardino area. Ten arduous hours behind the wheel yield a mere three hundred miles of progress.

By the time evening descends, I make the decision to seek respite at the nearest refuge, a Best Western that welcomes pets with open arms. As I settle in for the night, the weariness of the road fades into a peaceful slumber, buoyed by the promise of rest and renewal.

Awakening to the gentle light of dawn, I find myself rejuvenated and eager to resume my journey, fortified by a hearty breakfast, courtesy of the hotel. With the hum of the highway beckoning, I set forth once more, toward new horizons.

As the miles roll by and the landscape shifts beneath my wheels, I find myself enveloped in the boundless beauty of Arizona. Amidst the breathtaking vistas, the car radio is eerily silent in its refusal to yield a signal. In the absence of chatter, my thoughts turn to Einstein, whose silent presence provides a profoundly simple comfort. In his wordless loyalty lies a profound truth—the purity of unconditional love, a bond unmarred by the complexities of language. Perhaps the key to a deeper understanding of love, unspoken yet profoundly felt, lies in the quiet companionship of dogs.

I silently traverse the breathtaking landscapes, captivated by the myriad faces of the desert unfolding before me. The desert whispers secrets to those who listen, its silent expanse punctuated only by the rhythmic cadence of the wind against my car. In this quietude,

The Silent Echo of My Childhood

nature itself is beckoning me to embrace its tranquility and find peace in its embrace.

In the solitude of the road, I confront the void left behind by the absence of my beloved husband—a silence that has echoed in the depths of my soul since his passing. Yet, along with the silence, there is also hope. For the first time in what feels like an eternity, I find peace in stillness, allowing myself the space to reflect, grieve, and begin the journey toward healing. As I press onward, I am filled with anticipation for the adventures that await me in New Mexico—a land steeped in history, culture, and the timeless traditions of the Navajo people. It is a journey that promises to be as transformative as it is unforgettable. New Mexico invites contemplation of the vastness of the Navajo lands, the layers of rock and sediments mirroring the complexities of our own lives and the chapters they contain.

CHAPTER FORTY-SEVEN

My Life in Florida

In the tranquil embrace of my new life in Florida, I embark on a journey of healing and rediscovery, traversing the winding paths of my past to find solace and renewal. My story is one marked by the silent echoes of childhood trauma, a tumultuous first marriage marred by domestic violence, the betrayal in the business world, and the profound loss of my beloved husband, Dan, a little over four years ago, and other members of my family. Yet, amid the shadows of grief, I have found glimmers of hope and new beginnings.

In the company of kindred spirits within a writer's club, I have forged new friendships and embraced the joys of my widowed life. Together with my daughter, I have embarked on a new venture, a small business that we proudly own and nurture. As I immerse myself in writing, my dreams unfurl before me like petals in a gentle breeze. The artistry of words has become my sanctuary, a haven where I can pour out the depths of my soul and weave tales of imagination.

Sylvie Larivière-Traub

I also find solace in my mosaic art and painting, indulging in moments of quiet reflection within the confines of my small studio. My bond with my daughter blossoms with each passing day.

Though the scars of grief may never fully fade, I have learned to embrace the bittersweet symphony of memory, cherishing the moments shared with those I hold dear. As I savor the aroma of freshly brewed coffee each morning, I am reminded of the countless conversations and cherished memories with Dan, who enriched my life.

For too long, I remained silent, stifled by the weight of my past. Yet, even in silence, echoes linger, shaping our thoughts and actions. Through the cathartic process of writing, I have found my voice and reclaimed my narrative, illuminating the shadows of my past with the light of acceptance and understanding.

As I navigate the complexities of life, I am reminded that healing is not a destination but a journey, one marked by courage, compassion, and the possibility of redemption.

EPILOGUE

A Word About My Father

Reflecting on my father's words and through my journey of grief, I've traversed a spectrum of emotions, each one more profound and intense than any I've experienced before. Amidst the tumult of sorrow and longing, I've gleaned invaluable lessons. Chief among them was the necessity of embracing the present moment with those we hold dear. The fleeting nature of time has become abundantly clear to me, a sobering reminder that every minute, every hour, every day is a precious gift not to be squandered.

This newfound perspective has prompted me to reevaluate my relationship with my father, a figure whose presence loomed large in my early years. Despite the tumultuous nature of our bond, marred by his violence and anger, I found myself at his bedside in his final moments. Seeing him so fragile and frail, I couldn't help but be overwhelmed by a wave of compassion and forgiveness. In that fleeting moment, as I whispered words of love and forgiveness into his ear, I felt a profound sense of liberation wash over me. My father died when I was twenty-five years old, and I had seen him once or twice since my escape from Carrefour Sylvie. I felt guilt and regret at his deathbed.

The forgiveness I extended to my father was a cathartic release, unburdening me of the pent-up anger and resentment that had festered for years. In its place blossomed a newfound love and appreciation for him, a recognition of the lessons he imparted and the love he bestowed upon me during our time together. The memory of him, his moments where he smiled at me, or with Coco going for an ice cream, his encouragement and belief in my potential still resonates deeply within me, serving as a guiding light through life's myriad challenges.

The exact words he used have blurred with time, but the feeling they left behind is still vivid. When he wasn't drinking, he had a way of making the world feel right, his kindness and warmth shining through like the sun breaking through clouds. I can still recall those rare, precious moments when he would look at me with clear eyes and a gentle smile, telling me that I was capable, smart, and talented. Those words, spoken with such sincerity, seemed to settle deep within me, like seeds planted in fertile soil. In the toughest times of my life, when everything else felt uncertain, it was his voice I heard in the back of my mind, reminding me of my worth and giving me the strength to keep going.

In the tapestry of life, we can choose to dwell on the dark smudge upon the canvas or seek the light that emerges from shadows. In the mosaic portrayal of my family, I choose to cherish the radiant hues that shine through the storm, focusing on the bright stars and not the fleeting clouds. In times of challenges, it helps to look at the right side of life. I still remember holding his hand and walking with him and how I looked at him with my four-year-old eyes. My dad was my hero, and the power of forgiveness has reconciled me with him.

The Old Piano, a Serenade of Love

Similarly, the memory of my mother is a cherished treasure nestled deep within my heart, serving as a constant reminder of her love and support. Despite the brevity of our time together, cut short by illness, her enduring presence continues to shape my journey, guiding me through life's twists and turns. I fondly recall the tender touch of her hands as she guided me through my formative years and the melodic strains of the old piano she played for me.

In moments of struggle and uncertainty, these memories of her embrace offer solace and comfort, providing a sense of calm amidst life's storms.

As I reflect on the legacies of my parents, I am struck by the profound impact of their love on my life. Despite their imperfections, their roots, now intertwined with mine, serve as a foundation upon which I build my own legacy, carrying forward their love for me as a guiding force through life's challenges.

LAWSUIT AGAINST THE YOUTH PROTECTION OF THE QUEBEC GOVERNMENT

In my memoir, I recount the harrowing experiences of solitary confinement and various forms of abuse that I endured while under the care of the Quebec Government's Child Protection Department in a children's detention center. These traumatic events were not isolated; many other children suffered similar fates between 1950 and 1970. I, along with others, became part of a significant legal battle—the largest of its kind in Canada—against the Quebec Government, related to the systemic mistreatment alleged to have taken place in provincial youth protection facilities during those years.

Abuse Allegations

On September 7th, 2023, the Superior Court of Quebec granted authorization for a class action lawsuit seeking damages from the government (represented by the Attorney General of Quebec) and sixteen integrated university health and social services centers. This legal action addresses the reported abuses that allegedly occurred in youth protection centers across Quebec since 1950. The criteria for joining this lawsuit are as follows (as stated the original court document deposited at the Superior Court of the Province of Quebec):

Sexual assault and/or placement in solitary confinement.

Confinement to rooms or cells.

Application of force, with or without mechanical restraints (such as straitjackets, handcuffs, or shackles), use of medication, or other chemical substances.

Encouragement to smoke.

The court appointed Eleanor Lindsay, who initiated the lawsuit in 2019, as the lead representative of all class members. Lindsay alleges that she endured sexual abuse and solitary confinement in two Quebec youth protection centers during the 1970s. The claimants are collectively seeking $500,000 in compensatory and punitive damages.

The lawsuit contends that the Quebec Government and the named centers are responsible for the widespread detention and abuse of children within these facilities. The plaintiffs are asking the Superior Court to hold the government and centers accountable and to award damages to all class members, including Lindsay.

These allegations draw heavily from investigative reports published in the mid-1970s by the Montreal Gazette, which highlighted the severe punishment of girls, often for minor infractions like coughing, having nightmares, or crying.

While the defendants have yet to be proven liable, the trial is expected to proceed unless a settlement is reached. The outcome will determine if and to what extent the Quebec Government and the involved centers will be held accountable for the suffering endured by so many children. It was a significant victory for all of us who survived these abuses to see the lawsuit move forward.

www.ingramcontent.com/pod-product-compliance
Lightning Source LLC
Chambersburg PA
CBHW060521080526
44586CB00012B/568